Baptism Ahead

a road map for young disciples

WALLACE R. SMITH

JUDSON PRESS
PUBLISHERS SINCE 1824
VALLEY FORGE, PA

Baptism Ahead: A Road Map for Young Disciples

A NOTE FOR ADULT LEADERS AND MENTORS Visit www.BaptismAhead.org to participate in an online community—including a secure social network for young disciples to share their journeys and ask questions and a wealth of additional resources for you as a teacher and mentor of youth! And don't forget to look for the e-book companion, *Baptism Ahead: A Leader's Guide,* available for download at www.judsonpress.com or through the BaptistmAhead.org website ($7.00, PDF).

Judson Press has made every effort to trace the ownership of all quotes. In the event of a question arising from the use of a quote, we regret any error made and will be pleased to make the necessary correction in future printings and editions of this book.

Bible quotations in this volume are from the New Revised Standard Version of the Bible, copyright ©1989 by the Division of Christian Education of the National Council of the Churches of Christ in the United States of America. Used by permission. All rights reserved.

Library of Congress Cataloging-in-Publication Data
Smith, Wallace R., Baptism ahead: a road map for young disciples/Wallace R. Smith.— 1st ed. p. cm. ISBN 978-0-8170-1551-0 (pbk.: alk. paper) 1. Christian education of children. 2. Christian education—Activity programs. 3. Baptists—Education. I. Title. BV1475.3.S59 2009
268'.432088286—dc22   2009017568

Printed in the U.S.A.
First Edition, 2009.

friends of
JUDSON PRESS
PUBLISHERS SINCE 1824

Become a Friend of Judson.
Visit www.friendsofjudson.org.

For Mom and Dad,

who have guided with love,

wisdom, and grace

For Christy,

as we share the journey

of faith and life in love

and

For our
daughters,
Hanna & Hollyn,

that one day

they may freely choose

to follow Jesus

contents

Bethel Baptist Church

Dear friend,

YOU ARE INVITED to be a part of Baptism Ahead, a new group for older elementary and middle school youth at Bethel Baptist Church! Baptism Ahead is a group for youth to explore questions of faith, questions about baptism, and what it means to be a follower of Jesus and share in the life and ministry of the church. Baptism Ahead is designed for you to be able to freely explore and freely choose how you will respond to God at work in your life.

Baptism Ahead will meet on Wednesday afternoons between 4:30 and 6:00 p.m. at the Bethel Baptist Community Center. Students in sixth through eighth grades who are involved in the after-school program, as well as students involved in the church, have been invited to participate. After talking with your parent(s) or guardian(s) about Baptism Ahead, please have them sign and return the enclosed permission form. You will note that the permission form includes a requirement that a parent or adult mentor will participate in conversations and homework with you throughout the next several weeks of Baptism Ahead.

I am excited to share this adventure of faith with you, as together we discover what it means to be a follower of Jesus!

In God's grace,
Pastor Chris and Ms. Marsha

Introduction

A NOTE TO THE READER: You are invited to join in this journey of discipleship and discovery! As a young person at an age of accountability, making your own decisions as you explore questions of faith, as you consider what it means to follow Jesus, I hope that you will find this book to be helpful.

Here is some information to keep in mind as you read this book. In each chapter, you will share in the conversations of three primary characters—Ava, Jamal, and their teacher, Ms. Marsha. Their conversations may be similar to some of the conversations about faith and the church that you may already have or will have with a parent, a teacher, a pastor, or another adult mentor in your life. This book is meant to be a conversation starter for you; it does not include all the aspects of discipleship, nor is it a comprehensive work even on values that make Baptists "Baptist." This book is a starting point to get you in conversation with others at home or at church, with friends, and online.

Other sections in each chapter will be directed toward you, often with questions or thoughts to ponder, activities, and yes, even homework (I promise there are no grades given—the work is designed to help you grow, to experience and explore aspects of faith in deeper ways). While you might be tempted to skip ahead to the conversations between the characters, I hope you will read and interact with each section as a part of your learning and enrichment.

You may be reading this book on your own or as a participant in a group or class in your church as you consider faith commitments such as baptism or church membership. Whether you are in a group of two or twenty, I hope you will share the questions and conversations of this book with at least one adult mentor who can help navigate the journey of faith with you.

You can also continue the journey at **www.BaptismAhead.org**. This is a safe website for you to share your experiences, ask the author questions, and have virtual conversations about faith and life with youth in a global online community! This website is another way to equip you as you share the journey of faith with friends.

As you are on a journey of discipleship and discovery, this book, along with your Bible, will serve as a sort of compass or GPS to direct your journey. The funny thing about maps and compasses is that it is up to the navigator (*you*) to use them to your advantage. You may notice signs or directions to consider along the way, but ultimately, your adventurous relationship with God is up to you!

God is with us on the journey!

CHAPTER 1

"Under Construction"

Images of God

I picture God as very big and tall and holy
and watching over all of us. —Kayla, age 13

I would describe God as an old courageous man
with a white beard and draped in gold. —Lucas, age 12

God is smart, amazing, forgiving, creative. —Carolyn, age 12

I think of light and hope. —Catherine, age 11¾

- How would you describe God?
- How has your image of God been formed and shaped in your life?
- How is your understanding of God still "under construction"?

Key Term
Image: How you see or imagine something in your mind, like a picture in your head; it may also make you feel a particular emotion.

Baptism Ahead

The bell rang, and it was as if the foundation of the building shifted when the entire student body sprang to their feet. The first day of school was officially over, and Jamal could feel both freedom and chaos in the halls of Kennedy Middle School. He barely dodged a swarm of eighth-grade girls as he weaved through the crowded hallway toward his locker. On his way out, he helped point a new sixth grader who had that deer in the headlights look in the right direction toward the kid's locker. Jamal felt good; he knew his way around, and he had helped someone along the way.

He hopped on the bus and found an open seat. The bus got him at least halfway to his destination: the Bethel Baptist Community Center. Jamal had been going to the after-school program there for several years, even though he really felt too old for the program. Most of the youth his age didn't come anymore, but his mom did not get home from work until after 6 p.m., and she insisted. "It's not you, Jamal, it's the neighborhood," she said.

Secretly, part of him was relieved that she made him go. As an older youth, he got to lead games with the younger kids. Besides that, last year the center had been given a video game system, and he was king of the Bethel video game universe.

Today was also the first day of a new group just for the older kids, Baptism Ahead, with Ms. Marsha. He had gotten a letter inviting him to participate, and even though he groaned when his mom signed him up for it, he was secretly glad that she was making him be in the group. He did have a lot of questions, questions that were hard to put into words, and maybe he would learn something.

"Jamal, get off my bus!" The driver startled him from his daydreaming. A few kids laughed at him. He ducked his head, feeling the blood rush to his face—he felt as if a spotlight was shining right on him, highlighting his every move for all to see. He scurried down the aisle and out the panel door of the bus. Jamal hated being in the spotlight.

He waited for the bus to go before crossing the street through the fog of its diesel fumes. It was a sunny day and a hot walk to the church. After the bus rounded the corner and rolled out of sight, he made his way down the sidewalk.

As the church steeple rose on the horizon, Jamal could hear the rising sound of jackhammers. The intersection in front of Bethel Baptist Church at 24th Street and Martin Luther King Jr. Drive had been under construction for the past several weeks, and as he crossed the street to the corner, Jamal watched the workers breaking away layers of concrete, hot dust rising from the hammering. He hurried past, down the sidewalk along the church to the side door that was the main entrance for the neighborhood center. Ms. Marsha was welcoming some new kid at the door. Jamal smiled when he saw her—a familiar face at the end of a crazy day.

▶ ▶ ▶

Ava was the new kid again. Her dad's job had been transferred again. They had moved in the middle of the summer, and her family had started attending Bethel Baptist Church only a few weeks ago. Her older sister was off to college. Now it was only Ava and her mom and dad in a new house, a new city, another new beginning.

Ava's mom was excited to hear about the after-school program at the church's neighborhood center, because she too was starting a new job. So today, on Ava's first day at a new elementary school, it was also her first day to come to the church's community center after school, at least until her mom could pick her up before dinner.

Last Sunday in church, Pastor Chris greeted Ava and her family at the back of the sanctuary. "On Wednesday, we are starting a new group called Baptism Ahead. It's a group for youth your age to learn more about what it means to be a follower of Jesus. Ava, is that something you would be interested in?"

"YES!" Ava blurted. "Actually, I wanted to be baptized this summer after going to camp, but we were moving, and…"

Ava's mom interrupted, "We wanted to get settled, and we weren't ready to transfer our church membership here just yet. Could she still participate in the group?"

Pastor Chris said, "Of course she can! Ms. Marsha will be your teacher."

The time between Sunday and Wednesday seemed like forever. All week, Ava had been thinking of questions to ask. The first day of school was a blur of new faces, new everything. "New" had become normal for Ava. What she was really looking forward to was this time of learning about discipleship and baptism. She was excited and nervous as she walked to the church.

Ava walked up the steps to the front door of the church, but the door was locked. Then she remembered. Pastor Chris had said on Sunday to use the side entrance, the one with the sign for the neighborhood center.

Ava hopped down the stairs and rounded the corner. As the dust from the street construction cleared, she saw Ms. Marsha waving to her, a warm smile on her face. Ava's insides had felt jittery all day, but now she breathed a sigh of relief and walked up to her new teacher.

"Ava, it is great to see you!" Ms. Marsha greeted her. "How was your first day of school?"

She remembered my name! Ava thought. Ava didn't know the teacher except for being introduced by Pastor Chris on Sunday, but she instantly felt able to talk to Ms. Marsha. That felt good.

Ava smiled. "Today was okay, I guess, like the other two times I had to go to a new school. I talked to some girls at recess and lunch, but they were just being polite, I think…"

As Ava talked with Ms. Marsha at the door, an older boy brushed past. Ms. Marsha reached out and gave him a high five! That stopped him in his tracks. "Ava, this is Jamal," Ms. Marsha introduced her. "Jamal, meet Ava!"

Jamal went from giving the teacher a high five to sheepishly offering his hand to Ava, with a nervous smile on his face and a shy "hey" from his mouth. He wasn't cold, just shy. *Or maybe just weird around girls,* she thought. Ava was used to meeting new people. "Hello, Jamal. It's nice to meet you!" Ms. Marsha led them both into the church.

■ Think of a time and place when you were the new kid. What did that feel like?

■ Have you ever moved from a familiar place to a new place, or transferred from an elementary school to a middle school or junior high school? When did that new place or school begin to feel normal, like you belonged, like home? What happened to make it feel that way?

■ What does it feel like to be really welcomed and included?

■ Both Jamal and Ava seem very comfortable around Ms. Marsha. Why do you think they feel this way?

► ► ►

Ava curiously looked around the large room. In one corner, a group of younger kids were playing duck, duck, goose. At another area in the room, some kids were at a table working on their homework, and an older woman was helping them.

Ava quickly figured out that she was one of the older people in the room, and she was a sixth grader. She wondered if anyone else her age came to the after-school program. Had anyone else signed up for the Baptism Ahead group? Her insides were feeling jittery again.

"Jamal and Ava, could you join me in the library?" Ms. Marsha invited. The church library was a little room adjacent to the large room, and a big window separated the two. Ms. Marsha could see what was going on with the other kids and volunteers, but they also had a quiet space to meet in. Shelves of dusty old books lined the other three walls. It smelled like a library, but it didn't look like the books were borrowed very often. There was a round table in the middle of the room, and comfortable chairs around the table. Jamal quickly learned that the chairs swiveled, and that brought a sly smile to his face. Ava spotted a rocking chair next to one of the bookshelves and made herself comfortable.

Ms. Marsha proclaimed, "Welcome to Baptism Ahead!"

Jamal looked at Ava and then at Ms. Marsha. "Uh…where is everybody else?"

Ms. Marsha replied, "Well, you may have heard the saying of Jesus in Matthew 18:20: 'Wherever two or three are gathered in my name, I am there among them.' Today, it looks like we are that three! I am glad that you both are here, and I know that God is with us, as well."

Ava raised her hand. "Yes, Ava?" Ms. Marsha asked.

"Well…I thought this was going to be more like a class. How can we have a class without more, um, students?" Ava continued, "I just thought I'd have a chance to meet more people."

"Well," Ms. Marsha responded, "other youth were invited, but the truth is, you two were the people who said yes to this experience. And this might be a good thing—think of this as a conversation, instead of a class."

Ms. Marsha had a genuine smile that somehow naturally soothed the doubts that Ava and Jamal were feeling. "Let's begin!" she invited, and she began to open a large book of artwork that was on the table.

▶ ▶ ▶

Images of God Share this exploration with a pastor, teacher, adult mentor, or parent.

■ If you were to draw an image of God, what would you draw?
■ Ask each other to share a description or understanding of God. We do not have one definite description of or image of God. How-

ever, there are many references in Scripture that give us a broader understanding of who God is and how God connects to people. Here are some key images of God to explore:

■ Genesis 1:26-27
■ Exodus 3:1-6
■ 1 Kings 19:11-13
■ Mark 1:9-11
■ John 1:1-18

Which of these biblical images of God were familiar to you? Which descriptions give you a new image or understanding? What other images of God can you find in Scripture? In art? From your conversation and exploration with a friend or relative?

► ► ►

Ms. Marsha asked, "How would you describe God?" Ava and Jamal were both curious to see the picture in the big book that Ms. Marsha was holding, but the book was open to a clean, blank page.

After a moment of silence, Jamal quietly asked, "Um, do you mean, what does God look like?"

Ms. Marsha pondered. "That might be part of your description of God, but your image of God might also include how you understand God's actions and relationships in the world and with you!"

Ava volunteered, "I guess I've always imagined God with a long white beard! Like a grandpa, or…well…Santa Claus…" She trailed off, a little embarrassed.

Jamal said, "Well, I remember seeing a painting of the Greek god Zeus, you know, old, but with big muscles and a lightning bolt in his hand. That's kind of what I think of."

Ms. Marsha offered, "I think those are both good images. But let's go further. What else would you include in your image of God?"

Ava added, "I like the story when Jesus is baptized and it says the heavens opened and a dove came down and a voice said, 'This is my Son, my Beloved.'" She continued, "It just feels...right."

Ms. Marsha encouraged Ava. "That is a good connection: what we feel about God helps shape our image of and understanding of God. Good!"

Jamal was frowning a little. "But like my grandma always says, 'God is watching you!' But she says it more like a teacher saying she's going to send you to the principal's office—uh, not that I would know anything about going to the principal's office."

Ms. Marsha laughed. "That feeling is just as important to explore, Jamal. Some people do have an image of God that might be more like a principal than like a warm, healing light. Over the next several weeks, our conversation will continue, and much like the construction we can hear on the street outside the church, our understanding of God and Jesus and faith and the church is, well, under construction. And together, we are building an understanding of all these things."

Even though they had questions, Jamal and Ava seemed to click with what Ms. Marsha was saying. Jamal was wondering what Ms. Marsha meant about including more in his image of God, and what it meant to follow Jesus. Ava already had many questions written in her journal. A big question she was thinking of right now was *How will I know when I am ready for baptism?*

Ms. Marsha continued, "Tell you what. As we continue to build our images of God, we are going to each draw an image or symbol of God and share our images with one another. Then, we are going to explore some Scriptures that describe how God is in relationship with people. After we talk about those Scriptures, we'll see if we want to make any additions or changes to our drawings before we add them to this book!"

Ms. Marsha began to flip through the pages of the big book on the table. Mixed among the clean, blank pages were prints of famous artists' images of God, along with drawings and creations from many different children and youth, clipped and pasted into the book. Some images were similar to one another; many were very creative and different. All of them were beautiful.

Jamal and Ava have many questions forming as they have begun to explore with Ms. Marsha. You will learn more about their questions and feelings in the chapters ahead.

■ What are some of your questions about God, Jesus, the church, discipleship, and baptism? Write those questions in the space provided below:

_____

_____

_____

_____

_____

_____

_____

Homework
1. Where does my image of God come from? What or who has shaped my understanding of God?
2. Create your own image or symbol that represents God. Use whatever you have: markers, crayons, or perhaps a drawing program on your computer. You could also make a collage using images and words from newspapers and magazines.
3. Revisit the Scriptures from the earlier section in the chapter as you continue work on your image.
4. Share these images with your adult mentor or parent. Discuss the questions about your image of God.

@ **BaptismAhead.org:** You can share your descriptions of God and interact with other Baptism Ahead readers. You may be able to upload a digital image or scan your artwork to the website.

CHAPTER 2

"Who Do You Say?"

Conversations about Jesus

Jesus is God's Son sent to save us from our sins. He saves us from our sins so that those who believe can live without regret of previous mistakes. —Emily, age 11

Jesus is my BFF and my helper. —Stephanie, age 12

Who do you say that I am? —Jesus

■ What do you believe about Jesus?
■ How does what you believe about Jesus change who you are?

Key Term
Soul freedom: This is the deepest freedom that God has given to every person—the freedom to know and embrace God's will for you as an individual.

Ava was glad that Wednesday finally arrived. She couldn't wait to get to Bethel Baptist, because Wednesdays were the days set aside for Baptism Ahead. She couldn't wait to talk to Ms. Marsha today—Ava thought she might burst!

Ava had been given a diary on her last birthday, and she was pretty good at writing in it once, maybe twice a week. She had written quite a bit in the weeks before the family moved, and through tears in the car after saying goodbye to all her friends. But then she had not written again in her diary, up until this past week. She found herself writing in it every night, writing down questions to ask Ms. Marsha and writing her thoughts about God.

When she arrived at the neighborhood center, Ava headed straight for the library. Through the open doorway, she could see that Ms. Marsha was getting some of the younger kids started on what looked to be a sticky craft project. Ava looked around the large room but did not see Jamal.

I wonder where he is? He's usually here before me, Ava thought. Wait! There he was, coming in from the darkened hallway that led to the rest of the church and the sanctuary. *What was he doing, sneaking around in the church?* Ava wondered.

Jamal looked around from the entry, thinking no one was watching. He had arrived early at Bethel and had been to his secret hideout. He thought, *Okay, it's not a secret hideout, just a special place,* a place he went to think, to be alone in the quiet, safe place of this church. He was not planning to share his special place with anyone.

He tiptoed over to the corner where some younger boys were playing a video game. Ava watched as Ms. Marsha went over and gently tapped Jamal on the shoulder. She couldn't hear what was being said, but she could tell that Jamal was not too excited about coming to group instead of playing a game. Reluctantly, he followed Ms. Marsha toward the library.

"Ava, it is good to see you!" Ms. Marsha greeted her with a warm smile. Jamal mumbled, "Hey," and headed for his favorite swivel chair. Ava wanted so badly to pull her diary out of her backpack and show it to Ms. Marsha, but she was not sure if the time was right.

Ms. Marsha began, "Last week we shared our images of God. Your homework was to write down questions you have about God and to share your thoughts and discoveries with a parent or other adult in your life. Can you tell me about your conversations or share some of the questions you came up with?" Jamal shrugged and looked down at his shoes. Ava's hand was already in the air.

"Go ahead, Ava, and since there are just the three of us, you don't need to raise your hand to share."

Ava didn't hold back anything anymore.

■ At this point in the story, do you identify more with Ava or with Jamal? Why do you feel that way?

■ In class or group situations, are you comfortable asking questions? Why or why not?

■ Do you feel you are able to share your thoughts, feelings, and questions about God or Jesus with other people? Who are you most likely to talk to about questions of faith? Why?

■ If you could ask Jesus one question, what would it be?

▶ ▶ ▶

That girl sure can talk, Jamal thought. Ava was asking questions on top of questions, but instead of giving Ava answers, Ms. Marsha was responding with questions, such as, "What do you think?" And, "How do you understand what Jesus meant when he said that?" And, "What would your answer to that question be?" Jamal was trying not to be noticed as Ava and Ms. Marsha were talking, but it was hard to be invisible with only three people in the room.

As he was staring out the window toward the younger kids playing in the large room, Ms. Marsha drew his attention back. "Jamal? You've been quiet today. Do you have any questions you would like to ask?"

"I don't know…" His voice trailed off. He did have questions. Jamal just didn't know how to put them into words. *Why was it so easy for Ava? And why were girls so bubbly when they talked?*

"Well, I have a question for both of you," Ms. Marsha smiled. "Actually, it's an important question that Jesus personally asked his closest followers, and we are going to read it together in the book of Matthew, chapter 16. Did you both bring your Bibles today?"

In a flash, Ava pulled a pink Bible out of her backpack and started opening it to the New Testament. *Figures,* Jamal thought. His face and ears felt hot. Ms. Marsha noticed that Jamal did not move toward his backpack and quickly slid her open Bible in front of him on the table. Ava didn't see it happen, and Jamal couldn't hold back a smile for Ms. Marsha.

She went over and grabbed an extra Bible off of a library shelf, and as she opened it, Ms. Marsha asked, "What can you tell me about the Bible? Jamal?" Jamal's smile stopped as his eyes grew bigger, and his face and ears still felt hot. Quietly he said, "Umm…the first book is Genesis?"

"Good! Tell me more." Ms. Marsha was smiling at him now.

Jamal's voice was a little stronger. "Well, I know that Matthew, Mark, Luke, and John are called the Gospels," his voice began to get quiet again, "but I don't know what that word means…"

Ms. Marsha helped Jamal. "You are right that those four books are the books we recognize as the Gospels, which means 'good news' and serve as the story of Jesus' life and ministry. As followers of Christ, we look primarily to the Gospels to learn about Jesus. But the whole Bible is important and valuable for us as the story of God and God's people, including us."

She now turned toward Ava. "Ava, what can you tell me about the rest of the Bible?"

It was Ava's turn to be a little quiet. "At my old church, we memorized the names of the Bible books. But I haven't really read the Old Testament. Not on my own, anyway. I mean, I've tried, but it's really hard."

Ms. Marsha nodded. "Ava, I've been reading and studying the Bible for a long time, and I can tell you, there are many parts of the Bible that are hard to read and understand! But there is something we can learn from reading and studying the Bible, especially with a group like this.

"We understand that many of the books of the Old Testament are the story of God's people leading up to the life of Jesus, and the books and letters that come after the Gospels help us to interpret and understand what it means to be followers of Jesus. So it is important that as followers of Jesus we become students of the whole Bible."

Ms. Marsha continued, "Let us begin today with one story from Matthew 16, verses 13 through 19. Jamal, would you be willing to read the verses out loud?" Jamal's ears and face felt hot again, but he was kind of glad to be asked to read. It seemed easier when the words to say were right in front of him. As he read the passage out loud, his quiet voice grew stronger.

▶ ▶ ▶

Rumors about Jesus

Now when Jesus came into the district of Caesarea Philippi, he asked his disciples, "Who do people say that the Son of Man is?" And they said, "Some say John the Baptist, but others Elijah, and still others Jeremiah or one of the prophets." He said to them, "But who do you say that I am?" Simon Peter answered, "You are the Messiah, the Son of the living God." And Jesus answered him, "Blessed are you, Simon son of Jonah! For flesh and blood has not revealed this to you, but my Father in heaven. And I tell you, you are Peter, and on this rock I will build my church, and the gates of Hades will not prevail against it. I will give you the keys of the kingdom of heaven, and whatever you bind on earth will be bound in heaven, and whatever you loose on earth will be loosed in heaven." (Matthew 16:13-19)

In this passage, we find one of the most important questions Jesus ever asks: "But who do you say that I am?" How would you answer that question? Imagine that Jesus is asking you! What would you say?

Can you imagine the setting for this encounter between Jesus and the disciples? They were in Caesarea Philippi, a town on the northern border of Israel, built against a rocky canyon wall, and the place where fresh water springs from the mountain and starts the Jordan River. Caesarea Philippi was also a city of the Roman occupation and the center point of several groups and cults with different religious beliefs. The town and the cliff wall were covered with statues to all kinds of other gods, and it is in this global crossroads setting, surrounded by distractions and differences (and a foreign army) that Jesus asks the disciples, "Who do others say that I am?" Then he asks, personally, "But who do you say that I am?"

Notice that Jesus did not give the disciples an answer or direct their words; he asked the question and let them freely answer what they believe. Jesus asks us the same question. It's not about what our parents believe, or what our friends believe, or what we have heard others say about Jesus. Who do *you* say that Jesus is? Who is Jesus for you?

Reflect and write about your response to Jesus' question for you: **"Who do you say that I am?"**

_____

_____

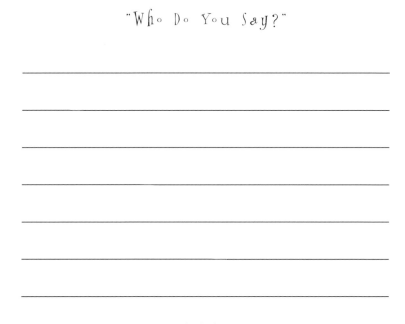

► ► ►

When Jamal finished reading the Scripture out loud, Ms. Marsha asked, "So...who is Jesus for you?"

Jamal looked for Ava to say something, but then he responded first. "Well, my mom has always said that she wanted me to know what it means for Jesus to be Lord and Savior. But I don't think I really know what that means...the only other lords I ever heard of were in history books about knights and kings and castles."

Ava giggled but nodded in agreement with Jamal. She added, "Those are words I hear in church, but at home, we haven't really talked about what words like 'Savior' and 'Messiah' mean. I had a friend who thought that Christ was Jesus' last name!"

There was a moment of silence, and Ava's smile faded. Then, her face showed frustration

Ms. Marsha asked, "Ava, what are you thinking about?"

Ava was quiet for a moment and then said, "Well, Jamal was saying that his mom talked to him about Jesus. I was thinking that with my mom and dad...we just don't talk about Jesus or faith that much."

"Do you feel that you could ask them some of your questions about Jesus?"

"I…I don't know." Ava was looking down at her hands. "I was just thinking that, well, I mean we go to church almost every week, but then during the week at home, we don't talk about church or Jesus. My dad says faith is a private thing, but I don't understand what he means."

Ms. Marsha's voice had a calming effect. "It is not easy for some people to talk about faith matters. It doesn't mean that they don't have a deep faith. Ava and Jamal, I want to encourage you to look for ways with your families that you can ask questions and explore what it means to be followers of Jesus with their help."

Ms. Marsha came back to her previous question. "Now, as for the rest of the time we have today, what I am really interested in is what *you* think! Who is Jesus for *you*?"

Ava replied, "Jesus is the Son of God!"

Ms. Marsha was still making room for Ava and Jamal to respond as they struggled with the question. "And…? What else would you say about Jesus? Jamal?"

Out of the silence, Jamal got serious. "Mom always says that the best role model I can have is Jesus, as a son, as a friend, even in my relationships with, uh, you know…girls. Mom says there is no better man to try to be like, so don't settle for anything less."

Ms. Marsha was listening closely to Jamal, letting him share his feelings as he was growing more comfortable.

Ava asked Jamal, "What about your dad?"

Jamal was quiet and then answered, "Umm…I never really knew my dad. My, well, my mom raised me by herself."

Ms. Marsha offered, "Well, your mom is a great mom, and she is absolutely right. There is no better person to be our role model than Jesus."

Jamal frowned a little. "But I *can't* be like Jesus, can I? I don't have super powers to make miracles. I don't even understand most of what Jesus is saying when he's telling stories." He paused and shrugged. "I guess I'm trying to say that I want Jesus to be my role model, but I don't know what it means to be like him…. So I don't even know if I answered your question, Ms. Marsha, but that's how I feel about Jesus right now."

Ms. Marsha smiled and patted Jamal's hand. "Today's conversation was not just about an answer to the question Jesus asks. While that is still important and I want us to continue talking about who Jesus is, what is important for you both to think about is your individual, free response to such a question. The value is to make your faith your own. Who are you in light of what you believe about Jesus? How has your growing faith changed you?"

Those were some big questions. Ava and Jamal were not sure what to say.

Ms. Marsha went on, "As a Baptist church, we believe in a fundamental understanding that God made each one of us with a free conscience, and each one of us has a freedom and a responsibility to choose how we respond to God and how we pursue our own relationship with God. We call this soul freedom. It is a big concept for us to understand, but it comes down to the question Jesus was asking in the Scripture today: 'Who do you say that I am?'"

Ava was the first to respond. "I never thought of it that way before…I guess I just thought there one right answer."

Jamal said, "I just thought my mom and people at church knew more than I did about Jesus, or that was why I didn't understand what my mom was saying about Jesus in my life."

"This is only the beginning of the conversation. There is so much more to explore!" Ms. Marsha encouraged them both. "So your faith is not just a copy of what your parents believe, or what the right answer is in Sunday school. Your faith is real when you take hold of it and say: This is what *I* believe! Do you understand?"

Both Ava and Jamal were nodding, but once again, there were more questions forming in their minds than answers forming in their hearts.

▶ ▶ ▶

This freedom means that *you* have the ability and the opportunity, the right and the responsibility, to form your relationship with God. While parents, mentors, teachers, and pastors may help form your faith, ultimately you are individually and independently responsible for you, your beliefs, and your actions. In our narrative, Ms. Marsha called this "making your faith your own." Later on, we'll explore how this freedom leads to Baptist beliefs regarding the ordinance of baptism, the ministry of each believer, and the freedom of the church as a community of faith.

Soul freedom
To our ears those words may sound odd. Yet they lie at the very heart of what makes us Baptists. Our belief in believer's baptism, in religious liberty, in the priesthood of believers— all the fundamental Baptist emphases—rest on the foundation of soul freedom. Simply put, it is the right and responsibility of each person to stand before God and make decisions about his or her relationship with God.
—Jeffrey D. Jones, *We Are Baptists: Studies for Older Elementary Children*, p. 1

■ What does it mean for you to be free?
■ What are the rights of freedom?
■ What are the responsibilities of freedom?
■ How is individual freedom balanced by life with a community of other free people?

"Who Do You Say?"

Homework

Before going further in the book, it is time for you to first do some research on concepts widely recognized as Baptist freedoms. With a parent or adult mentor, find a book about Baptists in your church library, or research the following phrases by using an online search engine or encyclopedia.

1. Soul freedom (also known as "the priesthood of all believers")
2. Bible freedom (also known as "freedom of interpretation")
3. Church freedom (also known as "autonomy of the local church")
4. Religious freedom (also known as "separation of church and state")

Together, discuss some of your findings. You may want to make some notes here:

_____

_____

_____

Throughout the book, we will explore how these freedoms are lived out in individual and community explorations of faith.

@BaptismAhead.org: Share your questions online! If you could ask Jesus one question, what would your question be?

And share an answer to the question: How is your personal freedom shaped by following Jesus?

CHAPTER 3

The Winding Way of Discipleship

To live your life for others. —Regan, age 14

To follow Jesus means to, in everything, do it through Jesus. To count on him for strength, and to let him lead you through your life. —Emily, age 11

■ What does it mean to be a follower of Jesus?
■ With whom do you share the path of discipleship?

Key Terms
Discipleship: A commitment to being a student or follower of Jesus; discipleship demands self-discipline to keep choosing what is right.

Bible freedom: You have the freedom to read and interpret (understand) the Bible yourself.

Ava was picking at her dinner, lost in her thoughts. "Hon, is something bothering you?" her mom asked. But Ava didn't respond.

Silence...then, quietly, Ava asked, "Why don't we talk more about God and Jesus?"

Awkward silence. "What I mean is, well...we go to church, but we never really talk about it after church. We pray at dinner at Grandpa's apartment, but we don't here at home. You say that you believe in God and Jesus, but we never really talk about them..."

Her mom and dad were looking at each other, stunned. Dad reached for the remote and turned down the volume on the evening news. More silence. Then Dad said, "Honey, your mom and I have always tried to give you a good foundation. We try to raise you like our parents raised us, and faith is a part of that. We do what we know, and so we go to church because that is what our families did."

Her dad put down his fork and thought for a moment. "I guess I've always been more private about these kinds of things when it comes to talking about it." He paused and sighed. "And I guess we don't feel that we know enough. We assumed that you would learn more from the pastor and from your discipleship class."

Ava reflected for a moment, still picking at the peas on her plate. "Well, I *want* us to talk about it. I want to know what you *feel* about things, not just what you *know* about things."

Ava's parents looked at each other and shared a smile. Her mom said, "One thing I do know, sweetheart, you are an amazing girl, and we thank God for you every day. Now, let's make a deal. You finish your vegetables, and we'll find something to have for dessert while we talk about anything you want."

■ Whom do you talk to about questions of faith?
■ Why do you think that talking about our faith is an important part of faith development?

■ What questions do you have that you have not yet shared with another person? Why haven't you shared them before?

▶ ▶ ▶

Jamal arrived early at Bethel. He looked around for Ava, but she had not appeared yet. He found Ms. Marsha reading her Bible in the library. He was glad to have a moment alone to ask Ms. Marsha a question. So without a hello or how are you, Jamal asked, "What does *disciple* mean?"

She turned to him and answered with a question. "Jamal! Good afternoon to you! Well, Jamal, let's look at the word itself. Can you think of any other words that are similar?"

He thought for a moment. "Ummm…it makes me think of 'discipline,' which is our principal's favorite word right after *Quiet!*"

"You are on to something, Jamal. And 'discipline' can mean following a set of outwardly or inwardly determined rules or setting certain boundaries. Discipline can also be about making difficult choices."

Jamal was paying attention to what Ms. Marsha was saying. She went on, "An example of self-discipline would be choosing something healthy to eat instead of choosing a sugary snack, or choosing to play outside instead of sitting on the couch watching TV—something inside you leads to your choice. Every day you are choosing a way of life as you determine your actions and activities."

Ms. Marsha stood and walked around the table, but her eyes were focused on Jamal's. "Now, think about some of the Scriptures we have read together. When the disciples ask Jesus a question, what do they call him?"

As Jamal was thinking about it, he hadn't noticed that Ava had walked into the room behind him.

"I know!" she interrupted. "The disciples call Jesus 'Master' or 'Teacher.'"

Ms. Marsha said gently, "Thank you, Ava, but I really wanted

Jamal to have a chance to answer the question. We're talking about discipleship today."

She continued to look toward Jamal. "So, in light of the disciples' descriptive words about Jesus, what else could you say about what it means to be a disciple?"

Jamal was quieter now that Ava was in the room, but he offered, "Well, I guess it's like a student, maybe?"

Ms. Marsha gleamed. "Great! The disciples are students of Jesus. And we, too, are students of Jesus. We are learning what it means to be followers of Jesus."

Ms. Marsha continued, "You both are showing an important sign of being good students. You are asking questions. Questions lead to more knowledge and understanding, but more than that, it means that we are learning from and with each other. Now, let's talk a little more about the discipline of being a good student of Jesus. And we are going to start by reading a part of a letter written by a teacher named Paul, to his student named Timothy."

▶ ▶ ▶
Students of Jesus

If you put these instructions before the brothers and sisters, you will be a good servant of Christ Jesus, nourished on the words of the faith and of the sound teaching that you have followed. Have nothing to do with profane myths and old wives' tales. Train yourself in godliness, for, while physical training is of some value, godliness is valuable in every way, holding promise for both the present life and the life to come. The saying is sure and worthy of full acceptance. For to this end we toil and struggle, because we have our hope set on the living God, who is the Savior of all people, especially of those who believe.

These are the things you must insist on and teach. Let no one despise your youth, but set the believers an example in speech and conduct, in love, in faith, in purity. Until I arrive, give attention to the public reading of scripture, to exhorting, to teaching. Do not neglect the gift that is in you, which was given to you through prophecy with the laying on of hands by the council of elders. Put these things into practice, devote yourself to them, so that all may see your progress. Pay close attention to yourself and to your teaching; continue in these things, for in doing this you will save both yourself and your hearers. (1 Timothy 4:6-16)

The apostle Paul is revered as one of the greatest teachers about what it means to be followers of Jesus. Many of the letters that Paul wrote to individuals like Timothy and to the earliest churches formed the structure and discipline and values of the church, and we look to these letters, a part of the Bible known as the Epistles, for guidance and instruction for the church today.

Paul was a mentor to Timothy, and it is believed by many that Timothy was a leader in the early church even when he was still a teenager. There are several references to Timothy being a youth and about his leadership in the church (see 1 Timothy 4:12).

This passage is also about the discipline of following sound instruction, leading by example, and "training in godliness" in comparison with the kind of physical discipline or exercise one might learn in gym class. While Paul is instructing his student, Timothy, there is also a clear reference in verse 16 that leads us to believe that the student is already a teacher to other people in the early church, learning from Timothy what it means to be a follower of Jesus.

You may want to read this passage with a friend or adult mentor and discuss these questions together.

■ What does it mean for you to be a follower of Jesus?
■ How are you a student of Jesus?

- How might you become a better student? What kinds of discipline might help, and what sources could you learn from?
- Do you feel you have permission to ask questions of faith? Why or why not? With whom do you learn about faith?

▶ ▶ ▶

As they were wrapping up their conversation for the day, Ms. Marsha offered a challenge to Ava and Jamal. "We've talked quite a bit today about what it means to be a student or follower of Jesus. Yet I hope you will remember this is not about getting the right grades with a Sunday school teacher or about any kind of test. What I mean is, discipleship is not something you do and then check off your list—it is a way of living and learning that becomes a part of who you are, every day, your whole life long."

Jamal was focused on Ms. Marsha. Ava was nodding in agreement. Their teacher continued, "As we end our time today, I want you both to consider two important ways that we continue to learn. The first is through our reading and understanding of the Bible, our best source to teach us what it means to be the people of God and to follow Jesus. You have the freedom to read and understand the Bible for yourself."

Ava looked puzzled. "What do you mean, for yourself? Do you mean by ourselves?"

"That is a good question, Ava!" Ms. Marsha winked. "You can read it by yourself, and I encourage you to, but can you two think of what might help you to read and understand the Bible?"

Ava offered, "I bet there are some books here in the library that could help us."

Jamal was being a little sly. "I think it's easier if you tell us what the stories in the Bible mean."

"Well, Ava, there are certainly many books that can help us interpret the Bible, and Jamal, I guess you might think it's easier if I were to tell you what I think, but then I would miss hearing what *you* think and understand about the stories of the Bible!"

Now Jamal was puzzled. "What could you learn from us?"
"Oh, there are treasures of feeling and understanding inside of each of you!" Ms. Marsha continued, "We each have the freedom to read and explore on our own, but our understanding of God's living Word is so much bigger and more complete when we share and explore and talk about it as a group, as a faith community!"

She went on, "We value community, and what it means for us as individuals to be involved in a way of life, together as God's people, learning from each other, caring for one another, and sharing the love of God with the world."

Ms. Marsha gave Ava and Jamal a piece of paper with a list of Scriptures and questions. "Now comes your favorite part! Homework! We are going to work on the discipline of Bible reading as a devotional, which means something we are devoting or committing ourselves to."

Ava was always excited about homework. Jamal was not showing excitement, but he was growing more and more curious with each discovery and each conversation.

▶ ▶ ▶

Bible Freedom

God created us with brains. We have the ability to think for ourselves. This freedom is an amazing and precious gift! How we use and live this freedom also carries a weight of responsibility. The Baptist understanding of Bible freedom, or freedom of interpretation, is one of the primary ways we live out the Baptist understanding of soul freedom, the freedom of the individual.

Just as you are reading this sentence and understand what you are reading, so you have the ability to read and understand the Bible. You can interpret the meaning of the stories and teachings of the Bible, as well. Understanding does not mean that you won't have more questions, and having the individual ability to determine meaning does not mean that you have to do it alone.

The Winding Way of Discipleship

Something important to remember is that you are not alone as a follower of Jesus! You share the journey with people who might have deeper wisdom and understanding from years of study and interpretation. You can share ideas and ask questions and learn together. That is where the church as a community plays an important role.

> Bible Freedom is the historic Baptist affirmation that the Bible, under the Lordship of Christ, must be central in the life of the individual and church and that Christians, with the best and most scholarly tools of inquiry, are both free and obligated to study and obey the Scripture.
>
> —Walter B. Shurden,
> *The Baptist Identity: Four Fragile Freedoms*, p. 9

Imagine if every person in your group, or family, or church were to each read the Bible but not share what you were reading and interpreting with one another. Isolated from one another, isolated from any other learning tools, you might come up with an interpretation of what the meaning of a particular verse or passage was, yet you would be missing some perspective on the whole story and not see connections between one teaching and another. So this is an individual freedom that is balanced with the participation in a larger community of individuals.

Almost every Baptist church has some sort of stated value about the Bible as the authoritative guide as the center of its church life. Yet churches and individuals have different understandings regarding how to interpret and apply the Bible in their living. Some believe in every story and word of the Bible as literally true. Others believe that the Bible speaks the truth yet believe that all the stories and histories included in the Bible don't have to be literally true to be meaningful. Some people claim that the Bible is God's Word, yet they rarely read the Bible, if at all. The point is that how we value the Bible is influenced by how we read and share the contents of what we believe to be God's Word. How do you read and explore and share the Bible?

It is also important to remember that the Bible is God's Word for us, and that is a living thing—not just a dusty old history book, but a way that God still speaks to us today. "The Bible is a record of God's Word in the past to be sure, but it points always to the future" (Everett C. Goodwin, *Baptists in the Balance*, p. 385). And each church and each individual has a right and responsibility to read and interpret and then apply shared learning and understandings in life together.

Bible Reading Tips

■ *Get a Bible you can read.* If you don't have a Bible of your own, talk to your pastor, parents, or mentor about getting one. Be sure it is appropriate for your age, such as a teen study Bible or a contemporary language version.

■ *Start simple.* Don't try to read the Bible from cover to cover. (I tried that when I was your age, and I don't think I made it past the third chapter of Genesis!) Start with one of the Gospels, and read one chapter each day.

■ *Reflect and ask questions.* It doesn't make much sense to keep reading if there is something that is not clear to you. Consider reading with a partner and discuss as you go along, or write down your questions and ask a parent, mentor, or pastor.

■ *Keep trying.* Reading the Bible does take effort (discipline). If you get bored or are having trouble sticking with it, find help, ask questions, read a different translation, or read smaller sections at a time. Be honest with yourself, and repeat these steps.

Homework

1. Talk to an adult in your life about what it means to be a follower of Jesus. What do you think it means? What does that adult think it means? Take turns sharing and listening.

Find what you have in common and where you may have different understandings.

2. Pick at least two Scriptures from the following list: Mark 1:16-20; Luke 9:23-26; John 8:31-32; Acts 11:25-26; 1 Peter 5:5-11. Read your selected Scripture through two times, and write down any questions or thoughts that come to mind.

3. Read the Scriptures again, but this time, as you finish reading, spend a moment in silence. What word or phrase from the Scripture comes to your heart and mind? Write the phrase down, and reflect on it.

4. End your devotional time with a time of prayer. Be sure to listen to God just as much as you talk to God!

@BaptismAhead.org: Share some of your own advice with online friends on how to grow in the discipline of Bible reading, study, and the discipline of prayer in your daily life.

You can also post a response to the question: What is hard about following Jesus?

CHAPTER 4

We Are God's People!

Exploring Faith Together

What I value about the church is that everyone is always so nice to me, helps and teaches me. The church helps me follow the right path! —Zach, age 10

[The church] is the key to a great life with God and Jesus. —Carolyn, age 12

Being comfortable with strangers because they are your brothers and sisters in Christ. —Nicholas, age 12

No matter who we are, God will always let us in his house. —Tim, age 11

■ What about the church is important to you?
■ A children's song reminds us that the church isn't just a building; it is the people. How would you describe your church?
■ What about your church would you like to change?

We Are God's People!

Key Terms

Community: A larger group with a common interest or similar values that works together for the good of everyone in the group.

Body of Christ: An image of the community of Christ followers that gives us a defining purpose: we are like the hands and feet of Jesus in the world today.

Church freedom: Just as you have individual freedom, the faith community also has a kind of freedom that helps the community work and act.

▶ ▶ ▶

Jamal's mom was tousling his hair. "Wake up, sleepyhead!" She could tell he was not asleep because he was frowning to keep his eyes shut.

"Mom!" He grumbled as one eye opened. "Why so early?"

"Jamal, remember, last week at church you signed up to be the youth helper for children's church! You need to be there with the teacher early today, before the kids arrive." His mom smiled. "I've even got breakfast ready for you as soon as you get dressed, and then we'll walk to church together!"

Jamal winced. "Walk? Too early!" But he was already springing up from bed.

Jamal was grousing on the outside, but he was awake and ready on the inside. He really did love playing with the kids at church. Now that he was old enough, Jamal could be a volunteer helper during children's church. He liked hearing the Scripture in the worship service and then hearing it shared in a different, simpler way with the younger kids during the story time at children's church. And it was fun to play and make things with the younger kids. It was like being an older brother.

Jamal hurried into his clothes, gulped his breakfast, and brushed his teeth so fast the brush hardly made contact. Now he was ready for church. He couldn't wait to get there.

► ► ►

Ava sat with her parents for worship. She might have to admit later that she wasn't paying complete attention during the sermon. But she hadn't been daydreaming. Not really, anyway. She was wondering where Mrs. Jenkins was today.

Mrs. Jenkins was the first person who had greeted Ava on the first Sunday they had visited the church. She was a frail woman, and she used a cane and always wore a hat to church. She smelled like flowers and had a sweet smile, and every Sunday she held Ava's hand when she asked Ava if she had a good week at school. Almost every week, Mrs. Jenkins would sneak a piece of hard candy into Ava's hand. Hard candy was not Ava's favorite, but Ava always said "Thank you" and ate the candy anyway.

Today, the pew where Mrs. Jenkins always sat was empty. And worship didn't taste like candy, either. It was like something, well, someone was missing.

At the back door following worship, Ava asked Pastor Chris, "Do you know where Mrs. Jenkins was today?"

Pastor Chris replied, "I don't know. Ava, thank you for asking, because you helped me remember to call her at home and see if she is okay."

As Ava walked down the church hallway with her parents, she heard singing from one of the children's rooms. She glanced into the room, and there was Jamal! And he was leading the kids in singing! It was an old song, one she remembered singing when she was younger at a vacation Bible school. "The church is not a building, the church is not a steeple, the church is not a meeting place, the church is the people! I am the church! You are the church! We are the church together!"

Later that evening, Pastor Chris called Ava at home. "Ava, I want to thank you again for noticing that Mrs. Jenkins was not in worship this morning. Mrs. Jenkins is all right. She did have an accident at home this morning while getting ready for church. She fell down and has a badly sprained ankle. Luckily, nothing was broken, but it looks like Mrs. Jenkins will be off of her feet for the next several days. I was wondering, would you and your parents be willing to take a meal over to Mrs. Jenkins tomorrow night?"

Ava quickly shared with her mother what had happened and what Pastor Chris was asking of them. Her mom said, "Of course," and so Ava told Pastor Chris that they would be happy to help out. When Ava hung up the phone, she was not sure what to feel. She felt badly for Mrs. Jenkins, but she also felt good that Pastor Chris asked her to help.

■ How are Ava and Jamal learning to become the church? How can people be the church?
■ How might you become more involved as part of your church's faith community?
■ What are some of the important values or practices of your faith community? (worship, youth group, specific mission activities)

On Wednesday, when Ava arrived at the Bethel Baptist Community Center, she gave Ms. Marsha a hug. Ms. Marsha was surprised by Ava's grip!

Ava rushed to explain. "Pastor Chris asked me if my family would take dinner to Mrs. Jenkins on Monday. "Mrs. Jenkins was so happy when we brought her the meal! Our whole family went over, and we ate dinner with her, and Mrs. Jenkins told all kinds of stories, and my mom and I did the dishes, and we brought extra food so we could put it in her refrigerator, and we're even going back tomorrow night to see how she is doing!"

"Wow!" Ms. Marsha responded. "I'm really proud of you, Ava! You know, this is one of the best parts of life in a faith community, taking care of one another and sharing life together. It is so important that you and Mrs. Jenkins and everyone else knows that no one is alone when we share the challenges of life as a community of faith!"

Jamal had walked up behind them as they were talking. Ms. Marsha patted Jamal on the shoulder and quickly brought him into the conversation as they stood together at the entrance to the church. "Jamal, thank you for volunteering to help this past Sunday with children's church and the younger children's Sunday school class! They really like having a teenager who plays with them! You are like a big brother to those children, and that is another great value of life in a faith community—serving others and teaching by example."

Jamal was embarrassed and proud at the same time. "Thanks, Ms. Marsha."

She then asked, "Jamal, what is your favorite part of working with the children?"

He thought for a moment, and then his face brightened. "Well, I really like it when I can see that one of the kids is learning something new. You can actually see it happen! And it is sort of fun to be the big brother."

Then Ava piped in, "And you can sing, too!"

Jamal wondered, *Was that a compliment, or was she teasing?* He remembered that she saw him singing with the kids. Jamal's only response to Ava was a little eye roll as they headed inside.

▶ ▶ ▶
The First Church

They devoted themselves to the apostles' teaching and fellowship, to the breaking of bread and the prayers.

Awe came upon everyone, because many wonders and signs were being done by the apostles. All who believed were together and had all things in common; they would sell their possessions and goods and distribute the proceeds to all, as any had need. Day by day, as they spent much time together in the temple, they broke bread at home and ate their food with glad and generous hearts, praising God and having the goodwill of all the people. And day by day the Lord added to their number those who were being saved. (Acts 2:42-47)

Some of the words included in this description of the early church are: *devoted, teaching, fellowship, breaking of bread, prayers, sharing, praising, glad, generous.*

■ What are the values and/or actions of the church that you see described in the Scripture?
■ Compare your church with the church described in Acts 2. What similarities do you see? What are some of the differences?
■ Which of the descriptive words from this Scripture describe your church? What other words would you add? What words would you *not* use? How do you feel about your description of "church," and what would you like to be different?

At the end of the chapter, you will be asked to interview your pastor. You may want to read this passage of Scripture together and share your observations about the values of the church with your pastor.

▶ ▶ ▶

As they walked into the library, Jamal and Ava both noticed that puzzle pieces were scattered over the large table in the middle of the room. "Are we having a play day?" Jamal asked, finding it hard to contain his excitement.

"Not exactly," Ms. Marsha smiled. "Today we are going to have a conversation about the church. We are going to explore what it means to belong to the church and how we all share in the ministry of the church."

"So…what's with the puzzle pieces?" Jamal asked, as he could not help himself from touching the pieces and looking for matching parts. Ava was clearly curious, as usual.

Ms. Marsha said, "We're going to play a game. Right now, let's focus only on the edge or border pieces. For each border piece that you match, I'd like you to name a group or a function or value of the church. For example,"—*click*—she matched two border pieces together. "We'll say that this piece represents the deacons, and this piece represents the prayer ministry team. Do you know what either of those groups does?"

Jamal shrugged, skeptical that this puzzle game was going to be any fun. Ava offered, "I don't know about the deacons, but my mom signed us up for the prayer chain, and we get calls at home from some lady who asks us to pray for people in the hospital or with an emergency, and then we're supposed to call another family."

Ms. Marsha congratulated Ava. "Good! That is a function of the prayer team. They also lead a prayer group that meets in the church each Thursday evening."

"Now, Jamal, could you tell me anything about deacons?"

He thought for a moment. "Well, my mom is a deacon. I know she has a lot of meetings at church. And she helps get Communion ready on the first Sunday of the month. My mom makes the bread fresh from scratch, and sometimes she lets me help cut it up for the Communion trays, and if there is leftover bread I get to eat it!"

Ms. Marsha gave Jamal thumbs up as she responded, "Okay, you are off to a good start. Our deacon board helps with some important functions of the church, such as helping with big decisions for the church and preparing elements for worship, like Communion. Our deacons can also help Pastor Chris with baptism. Now what else do you think that our deacons do?"

Jamal squinted in thought. Then he added, "Well, one time when Mr. and Mrs. Jackson were in a car crash, they had a room together in the hospital. My mom took me with her when she went to visit them. Actually, she goes to visit lots of people, but I don't know if that's because she's a deacon or because she just wants to."

Ms. Marsha smiled her knowing smile. "I bet it's both because she is a good friend and because she is a deacon. The deacons do represent the whole church family when visiting people in the hospital and others who are homebound or in nursing homes. That is a simple thing we all can do, and one way we take care of each other as a church family."

Ava asked, "Why are there so many meetings at church? I mean, in the bulletin I always see lists of meetings. My dad says board meetings should be spelled b-o-r-e-d."

Ms. Marsha tried to swallow a laugh. "Well, Ava, I guess some meetings can seem b-o-r-i-n-g. We do talk a lot. But the meetings at church are important. Many people are involved in the decisions of the church."

"Like what?" Ava asked.

"Well, like what we do for ministry in the neighborhood, including the after-school program, or what we do in ministry with children on Sundays and throughout the year. We have another group that plans ministry with our senior citizens. And we have a missions group that determines how we can best use the resources of our building and our worship offering and people for mission and ministry in the community."

Ava thought for a moment. "I guess I just thought that the pastor was the boss of the church. I thought Pastor Chris did all those things."

Ms. Marsha was smiling again. "Ava, in most churches, and especially in Baptist churches, we really value making decisions together. All members can have a say in our decisions and can participate in the work, too! Remember when we talked about how we value the freedom of each person?"

Ava was nodding. "I guess we wouldn't be free if the pastor just told us what to do!"

Ms. Marsha went on, "We will keep talking about how that freedom works in our life together as a community. It is not always the easiest way, in a group that can have many different ideas and opinions. But it is a good way."

Ms. Marsha pushed some puzzle pieces toward Jamal and asked. "Now, Jamal, can you think of any functions or actions of the church?"

Jamal grabbed an edge piece and looked for a match. "Well...what about worship? And," he found a match and clicked the pieces together, "Sunday school?"

"Great!" Ms. Marsha encouraged. "Now what questions come to mind for either of you regarding worship or Sunday school?"

Ava jumped at the chance to ask a question. "I have one. Who decides what the subject is or the songs we sing each Sunday? Or does Pastor Chris get the order out of some big book?"

Ms. Marsha was impressed by the question. "As Baptists, we are a part of a free church tradition. Just as we value the freedom of the individual, we also value what we call church freedom. Our church has the freedom to plan our worship as we determine. We have a worship planning team that discusses Scriptures and themes and plans our schedule of worship. So several people share in the work of planning and leading worship. We will talk more about worship later on, but let's add some more pieces to our puzzle."

As they continued to work on the puzzle, Jamal, Ava, and Ms. Marsha shared ideas and asked questions about different aspects of the church. With each puzzle piece—*click*—new questions came up about church membership, missions, serving the poor, the after-school program, children's ministry, church committees, Bible studies, and classes, among others. Together, they determined the corner or foundation pieces as representing God, Jesus, the Holy Spirit, and the Bible.

▶ ▶ ▶
Church Freedom

The document we know as the Declaration of Independence was written in 1776 and is considered to be not just an important guiding document in the formation of the United States but has been referred to throughout the past three centuries by groups around the world seeking similar values of freedom and equality. It begins with those famous words: "We the people...in order to establish a more perfect union."

If as a church we were to write a new yet similar document to share what we value and what unites us with one another (such as freedom in Christ, as reflected in Galatians 3:26-28), we might start with the words "We God's people." We would write about the freedom of the individual and the freedom of the church as a community, in relationship to the wider communities, states, and countries in which we live.

Baptist churches recognize and value the freedom of the local church. As they recognize soul freedom, the freedom of the individual, Baptists recognize that each church is individual and independent of systems and structures that would otherwise tell the church what to do: how to worship, who to choose as pastors and church leaders, how to participate in ministry in the community and wider world.

■ Have you ever visited another Baptist church (besides the one that you already participate in)? How was that church different from your church? How was it similar?

_____

_____

_____

Every church has the right and responsibility to choose how to worship, how to involve people as participants in worship, what kinds of songs to sing, even what time to worship and for how long (some church services are way longer than others!).

■ How does your church plan the worship service and involve participants in worship?

_____

_____

_____

Every church has the right and responsibility to choose how it organizes programs and ministries, from decisions about who serves in leadership to rules (bylaws) about membership, voting rights, and decision making. Because of our belief in soul freedom, most Baptist churches function as a democracy, where the individual members have a voice and a vote. The pastor is elected as a servant leader, and ultimately the power of how the church is governed belongs to "we God's people"—and that means everybody.

■ What kinds of rules and structures does your church have in place regarding church leadership, church membership, and decision making in the church?

_____

_____

_____

■ What kinds of groups (committees, business meetings) make decisions in your church, and how are those people chosen or elected to be leaders in your church?

_____

_____

_____

While Baptists value freedom and independence, from our earliest history, individual Baptist churches chose to associate together in common mission. They agreed to be partners and share human and financial resources to accomplish bigger things for God. An example from the 1700s in America: several churches worked together to send Adoniram and Ann Judson as missionaries to what is now known as Burma. These churches met together, prayed together for the missionaries, and raised money for a ship and supplies for the Judsons to do their work overseas.

■ Can you name some of the ways your church chooses to partner with other organizations in mission? If not, find out what partnerships of associations your church has with other congregations or organizations in the area. Ask about which mission efforts or individual missionaries your church supports across the nation or around the world.

_____

_____

_____

▶ ▶ ▶

As they finished the border of the puzzle, Jamal was curious. "So, what about the center pieces?"

Ms. Marsha winked. "Well, I was hoping you would ask! While the programs and ministries and values of the church may help define and give shape to the church, we know that the picture is not complete without what really makes up the church! Jamal, what have we not yet talked about when it comes to our picture of the church?"

He thought for a moment and asked, "Do you mean the people?"

Ms. Marsha encouraged him, "You've got it! The church is the people! Let's name different people that we know in our church family with each piece that we place."

Going in a circle, starting with Ava, each of them named people as they placed pieces: "Mrs. Jenkins"—*click*—"Andy the janitor"—*click*—"Joan Wilson"—*click*—"my mom"—*click*—"Mr. Price"—*click*—"Ava!"—*click*—"Pastor Chris!"—*click*—"Jamal!" —*click*—"Ms. Marsha!" Slowly, the picture of the puzzle came into full view. It was an artist's image of Jesus. Jesus was smiling.

▶ ▶ ▶
Membership: Belonging
Church membership is a way that churches officially recognize a person's commitment to be an active part of a faith community. Baptist churches can have different definitions and expectations of church membership. (In your homework, you will explore the meaning and expectations of membership in your church.)

■ Read Ephesians 4:1-6. What does this Scripture say to you about what it means to belong?

_____

_____

■ When you have a group of free people, you can have many different ideas, values, opinions, and attitudes. What would unity look like in a diverse group of people?

_____

_____

_____

■ Read Romans 12:4-13. What do you think this Scripture is communicating about what we do or how we function together as the body of Christ?

_____

_____

_____

■ The body of Christ is much larger than just your church. Who else belongs in the body?

_____

_____

_____

Homework

Interview your pastor. Review the description and questions regarding the early church from the previous section in this chapter. Then set up a time to meet with and interview your pastor. Ask your pastor to share how he or she understands the values of worship, mission, and community as reflected in Acts 2:42-47, and share your observations with your pastor, as well.

Other questions to include in your interview:

■ What does it mean to be a member of the church?
■ How do members share in the ministry of the church?
■ How does our church share in ministry in the community and with other churches?

What questions would you like to ask your pastor? Write those questions in the space provided below:

_____

_____

_____

_____

_____

_____

@BaptismAhead.org: Share your definitions of church and what it means to belong to the body of Christ.

CHAPTER 5

At Water's Edge

Exploring Believer's Baptism

I was baptized in seventh grade, and I made the decision after taking a class at my church that taught me that Jesus loved me and welcomed me with open arms. I had a mentor who would meet with me and help me to make the decision. It was a very exciting day! —Amy, age 14

I took a Faith Steps class and I made a banner that had my favorite Scripture on it. Then on the day of my baptism they talked about my life at church. After all of that I felt like I was a new and better person inside. —Natalie, age 12

Well, my friend Kayla and I were baptized on the same Sunday. I was so excited that I thought my heart was going to EXPLODE OUT OF MY CHEST! My family and my friends were all there to support me! My body and soul now belong to Jesus, and I'm looking forward to the next part of my journey. —Zach, age 10

Baptism Ahead

- What do you understand about the meaning of baptism?
- Have you made a commitment of faith to Jesus?
- Do you think you are ready for baptism? Why or why not?

Key Term
Believer's baptism: A ceremony of the church in which a person who has declared personal faith in God makes the decision to be baptized (usually by immersion in water, which means the person being baptized goes all the way under the water) as a symbol of change in his or her life and a desire to follow Jesus.

▶ ▶ ▶

Jamal was nervous as he rode the bus home from school. His stop was the second to last one on the east route from Kennedy Middle School, and usually on the long route, even in the excited buzz of other voices on the noisy bus, he still found time to get the easy part of his homework done. Not today.

He had been enjoying the after-school conversations with Ava and Ms. Marsha. It was safe to ask almost any question with Ms. Marsha, and he felt he had learned a lot. But today was the day they were going to talk about baptism. He did not want it to show, but just thinking about it made his stomach feel all twisted.

He was not afraid of the water. It was the thought of all those people who might be in the sanctuary on some future Sunday morning, with their eyes on him. Why did it have to be so...so...*public*? What if he said the wrong words?

What if he got water up his nose like that fifth grader, Brian, at the last baptism Jamal witnessed in church? That kid sputtered and choked, and some people couldn't help but laugh. Being in front of a crowd like that, feeling so vulnerable? That just was not cool. *Okay, maybe I am afraid of that kind of water, and being in public.*

But was that it? Was that what was bothering him? Or was it something else? Maybe he wasn't ready to talk seriously about this whole baptism thing.

What was baptism really about, anyway?

The bus driver was yelling now: "Hey, Jamal! Let's go! Quit daydreaming! I got another stop to make, pal!" Jamal was startled, dropping his backpack as he swung out of his seat. A voice from behind him chuckled: "Yeah, wake up!"

Some kids in the back started laughing. *That's just great,* Jamal thought as he looked down, brushed past the driver, and hopped off, on his way toward the Bethel Baptist Community Center. It was usually a long walk from his stop to the center. *Not long enough today,* he imagined.

► ► ►
Origins of Baptism

John the baptizer appeared in the wilderness, proclaiming a baptism of repentance for the forgiveness of sins. And people from the whole Judean countryside and all the people of Jerusalem were going out to him, and were baptized by him in the river Jordan, confessing their sins. Now John was clothed with camel's hair, with a leather belt around his waist, and he ate locusts and wild honey. He proclaimed, "The one who is more powerful than I is coming after me; I am not worthy to stoop down and untie the thong of his sandals. I have baptized you with water; but he will baptize you with the Holy Spirit."

In those days Jesus came from Nazareth of Galilee and was baptized by John in the Jordan. And just as he was coming up out of the water, he saw the heavens torn apart and the Spirit descending like a dove on him. And a voice came from heaven, "You are my Son, the Beloved; with you I am well pleased." (Mark 1:4-11)

Baptists trace the Christian practice of baptism back to the example of Jesus, who was baptized by John the Baptist in the Jordan River at the beginning of his public ministry. But what did this symbolic act of baptism mean to Jesus? Some would recognize his baptism, and the subsequent parting of the heavens and voice from God, as a public anointing and as God's blessing on Jesus at the beginning of his ministry. Some of the students, or disciples, of John the Baptist recognized this baptism as a sort of passing of the torch to Jesus, and they left their old teacher to become disciples of Jesus. John the Baptist had made it clear that he was not the Messiah but the one who pointed the way to Jesus, who was the Messiah. The Messiah, or Savior, would save God's people.

But where did John the Baptist come up with the idea that immersing people in water was a way to change their life? Biblical historians trace this baptism of repentance to a community that John the Baptist may have lived in and been a part of before going out into his own ministry in the wilderness. They were called the Essenes, and they were a group of religious people who lived apart from the rest of the Jewish community. More than anything, they wanted to be faithful to the Jewish Scriptures. One of the symbolic acts they shared was a regular (perhaps daily) ritual washing of their bodies that symbolized their desire for purity before God.

John the Baptist spoke of a baptism for the forgiveness of sins. Perhaps you have heard a similar phrase in a song during worship or heard someone say something like, "All my sins were washed away." You can trace the meaning of that all the way back to the baptisms we find recorded in Scripture.

Yet even John the Baptist said, "I baptize with water, but Jesus baptizes with the Holy Spirit." John was clear that the water itself did not save a person. The real power came with the baptism of the Spirit, something that comes only from God through Jesus. What a beautiful image for us, to be immersed in the Spirit of God!

Baptism is a special action, a symbolic way for us to connect with and follow the example of Jesus. It is an act of humility and a symbol of our desire to repent, to turn away from one direction of living and turn toward a life of choosing daily to follow Jesus.

Paul believed that baptism was symbolic of dying and rising into new life, a different life from the life we lived before we knew and accepted Jesus as Lord and Savior. Paul went on to say that our baptism connects us to Jesus in a special way.

■ How might you interpret what Paul says about baptism in Romans 6:1-5? Read this passage and write your thoughts here:

_____

_____

► ► ►

While Baptists have traditionally baptized people by immersion instead of sprinkling or any other form, it's not about the water or the amount of water. Here is the most important thing to understand about the Baptist practice of baptism: what matters is that the person being baptized is old enough to understand what it means to follow Jesus and freely choose Jesus as Lord and Savior. This expectation is directly connected to the Baptist value of soul freedom, the belief that every individual has the freedom and responsibility to choose to follow Jesus. One's authentic faith can not be coerced (manipulated or controlled) by any other person.

Believer's Baptism

In Baptist life,…followers of Christ make a public statement of their faith through the waters of baptism. Ask the average person what is the distinguishing characteristic of [a] Baptist denomination, and they will probably answer with something about the *way* Baptists baptize. While true today that Baptists universally practice baptism by immersion, their earliest concern regarding baptism was not the *mode* of baptism or *how* one should be baptized. Their earliest concern was...*who* was being baptized. —Walter Shurden, *The Baptist Identity: Four Fragile Freedoms*, p. 29

For faith to be real, it is freely explored and freely chosen by each person. Your faith is not a clone of your parents' faith, or your pastor's, or any other person's. While those who teach and guide you may influence what you believe, ultimately, it is up to you. What do you believe about God? What do you believe about Jesus? How do you read and understand the Scriptures? How do you choose to live in connection to the faith community that is the church? Are you ready to follow Jesus? The symbol of your yes to Jesus is to follow him into the waters of baptism.

This is a great time to pause in your reading and talk with a parent, mentor, or pastor about what it means to follow Jesus and to ask your questions about baptism. You can write your questions online at www.BaptismAhead.org.

_____

_____

_____

▶ ▶ ▶

Even though Jamal had taken his good sweet time between the bus stop and Bethel Baptist, he still had the butterflies in his stomach.

"Here we go," he muttered to himself as he rounded the corner to the side entrance that connected the sanctuary part of the church building to the community center. Kids of all ages were trickling in to the different after-school activities in the big room and in rooms off the main hallway. But today Jamal was headed to meet Ms. Marsha in the church library for their weekly Baptism Ahead conversation. The door was open, and he took a deep breath and exhaled as he walked in.

Ava was already in the rocking chair, her favorite spot, and waved as Ms. Marsha stood up and welcomed Jamal. Ms. Marsha asked, "How was your day?" Her knowing eyes could see that Jamal seemed to be carrying more on his shoulders than the weight of his backpack.

"Fine," he mumbled as he crumpled into the swivel chair opposite Ms. Marsha and Ava. He wasn't going to offer any more than that, as he crossed his arms and looked down.

"Well, I am glad you are here," Ms. Marsha smiled, leaving Jamal some time and space to warm up to the conversation.

"Can we talk about the homework we had on Acts 2:42?"

Ms. Marsha assured Ava, "We'll talk about your homework from our conversation last week a little bit later, but right now, let's go on a little field trip." With that, she led Ava and a reluctant Jamal out of the office and down the hallway to a door that opened to a flight of stairs.

From the best that she could navigate, Ava said excitedly, "I think this goes behind the sanctuary!" She was right, for as they got to the top of the stairs, another set led back down and into what looked like a small, empty swimming pool with an open window looking over the sanctuary. Ms. Marsha said, "I thought this would be a good place for us to talk about baptism!"

Ava was excited. "I can't wait to be baptized!"

Ms. Marsha asked her, "What does baptism mean for you, Ava?"

Ava reflected for a moment and then said, "I've talked to my parents about it, and you both know that neither of them have talked much about their own beliefs, but this time it was different. They wanted to hear what I had to say. I told them that for me, baptism was my way of telling the world that I wanted to follow Jesus and live like Jesus and let God lead my life."

Jamal was listening closely. Ava was almost two years younger than he. How was she so sure of what she believed? Why was she able to say how she felt when he still felt nervous and confused?

Ava was smiling with joy as she continued, "My dad says he was raised Catholic, even though he never talks about it much, and I don't remember him ever telling any stories about church from when he was younger. He was baptized when he was a baby. When we were talking the other day, he did say that he went to classes when he was our age—cataclysm or something."

Ms. Marsha couldn't hold back a little chuckle. She gently corrected Ava, "That's catechism. It's just a big name for what we are doing with this discipleship group, learning about our faith and what it means to live that faith. Different faith traditions have different ways of confirming and teaching important aspects of faith."

Ava went on, "Anyway, my mom grew up going to church and got baptized when she was ten after going to a church camp, but even though after she left home and didn't go to church much after that, she and my dad started going to church together after they had me. And while we've always gone, we just never talked much about it until now."

Ava took a breath and kept going. "These past few weeks since we have been talking here, my parents have listened to me but say things like 'That's nice' and go on reading the paper or whatever. This week, though, when I talked with them about baptism, we really got to talking!"

"That's great, Ava!" Ms. Marsha encouraged her. "It sounds like you are just about ready to tell the whole church what you already know in your heart."

Ava stopped for a moment, curiously looking around the tiled baptistery to a faucet and down at the drain in the floor. "Um, Ms. Marsha? I do have a question, though. This may sound silly, but exactly how does it work? It's just, I know what it means, but, the only thing is, how do you put someone under water without water getting up their nose or something? And how deep is the water? I don't really like deep water."

Ava added, "I can barely see over the window into the sanctuary."

Jamal was listening with curiosity. He was thinking, *Ava's nervous about the water! Maybe I am a little afraid of the water, too.* Earlier, he was just thinking about that kid Brian who got water up his nose and the crowd watching him. But now he was imagining this place where he was standing full of water. Jamal's face was like stone, but his stomach was feeling pretty shaky.

Ms. Marsha was encouraging. "Well, that is part of why we are here, to let you see how we do baptism and ask exactly those kinds of questions. The water will be warm, like a pool, and will seem like the shallow end of a pool, up past your belly button, but you will be able to stand. If someone is a little shorter, we have a block that they can stand on. Your feet will remain on the floor of the baptistery. Pastor Chris will stand behind you and ask you, 'Do you believe that Jesus Christ is your Lord and Savior?'"

Ms. Marsha was looking at Ava and Jamal. "What do you think happens next?"

Jamal shyly said, "I think we're supposed to answer yes."

"And then, as you stand in the water, the pastor will say, 'Upon your profession of faith, I baptize you in the name of the Father, and of the Son, and of the Holy Spirit.'"

Ms. Marsha encouragingly put her arm around Ava's shoulders. "Here, Ava, let me show you." Ava jumped forward but was still a little nervous.

As Ms. Marsha spoke, she demonstrated to Ava how the pastor would hold on to her in the water. "At that point Pastor Chris will hold one arm behind you and the other hand right at the top of your chest at your collar bone. Or, if you prefer, the pastor can hold a cloth handkerchief over your nose and mouth if you are really nervous about water going up your nose. Then Pastor Chris will lunge to dip you backward into the water, and right back up! Would you like me to demonstrate?"

"Without water?" Ava asked. "How will you do it?"

"Even without the water, I can hold you," Ms. Marsha said. "It will be sort of like a dancing move, and I can support your weight. It will be even easier with the water! Here, let me show you."

Ms. Marsha held on to Ava and dipped her backward. They practiced while Jamal watched. After practicing with the teacher, Ava felt excited again. But she asked, "Ms. Marsha? Will the pastor remember to cover my nose?" Ms. Marsha winked and smiled, "Yes, I will remind Pastor Chris myself."

"How about you, Jamal?" Ms. Marsha asked. Jamal looked a little wary. "Uh…I think I'm too big for you to try it without water in here."

Ms. Marsha reassured him. "Well, if it would help you feel more comfortable, you could just step with one foot backward while I dip you. We can do it with teamwork! Jamal, I promise you I won't drop you, and I won't let go."

Jamal was reluctant, but he halfheartedly practiced with Ms. Marsha. He was surprised, but she was right. She did not let go.

▶ ▶ ▶

Reflections in the Water

Baptists believe that baptism "is an outward sign of an inward and invisible presence of grace" (Everett C. Goodwin, *Down by the Riverside: A Brief History of Baptist Faith*, p. 85). In other words, we believe that believer's baptism is a way for us as disciples of Jesus to show the church and the world about how God has already touched and changed our lives through Jesus.

Scripture has had a big influence on how Baptists think about baptism and what it means in our life of faith. Biblical stories of Jesus' baptism can be found in Matthew 3:1-17 and in John 1:29-24, but today, read Luke 3:1-22 and consider the following questions.

■ What do you think the action of baptism symbolizes as it is shown in Luke 3:3? What does that mean for you?

_____

_____

_____

■ In verses 10-14, different people ask John the Baptist, "What then should we do?" Why do you think that is an important question for a person who has made a new commitment of faith?

_____

_____

_____

■ How do you think you might you live differently because of your faith commitment?

_____

_____

_____

Take a few moments to read verses 21-22 again, and then close your eyes and imagine the sky opening, the Spirit appearing "like a dove," and hearing God say, "You are the Beloved; with you I am well pleased." Can you hear those words for yourself? I hope that you know you are God's beloved and that you bring joy to God!

▶ ▶ ▶

After they practiced, the three sat down in a circle on the dry floor of the baptistery. Ms. Marsha shared, "We've been talking about what it means to follow Jesus, about the church, and about your questions of faith. And you both seem to understand that it is about your free, personal commitment, lived out in relationship with others. Baptism is a symbol of that commitment."

Ms. Marsha paused, letting her words sink in, and then continued, "But your baptism is not about the water. It is about your heart and soul and mind. We baptize with water, a symbol of entering a new life, but God baptizes you with something we can't see but *can* know. That God's Spirit is in our hearts. Because of our faith commitment, we freely choose every day to follow in a life of love that reflects the love and grace of God. When you are ready for this kind of commitment, you are ready for baptism."

Ava almost shouted, "I'm ready!" Jamal's eyes met with Ms. Marsha's, but he didn't say a word. She smiled and gently offered to pray with them before they left the baptistery. "Dear God, thank you for this time that we have had together to talk about baptism. More than that, thank you, God, for telling us that we are your beloved children. Thank you for your love and grace. May you continue to be at work in Ava and in Jamal, as they consider what it means to be your beloved children and consider baptism as a symbol of their commitment to follow Jesus and to live as your beloved children. In Jesus' name we pray, and we live! Amen."

Jamal stayed quiet. At least Ms. Marsha hadn't put him on the spot. He had talked with his mom, and she wanted him to be baptized, and he didn't want to disappoint her. But after listening to Ava and Ms. Marsha, he didn't feel ready yet, whatever "ready" meant.

Homework

1. Read and reflect on some stories of people making faith commitments and their choice to be baptized, as found in the book of Acts, which describes the life of the early church: Acts 8:12-13; 8:36-39; 16:29-33; 18:8.

2. Discuss some of these questions with your pastor, parent, or adult mentor:

■ Can you tell me what you remember about your baptism? What does baptism mean for you?

■ Do the members of our church believe that one has to be baptized to be a member or to share in the Lord's Supper (Communion)? Why or why not?

■ Do the members of our church recognize other forms of baptism besides immersion (such as sprinkling or pouring water over the head, or the pastor touching the person with water)? Why or why not?

■ If people who were baptized in another church tradition (such as being baptized as an infant) have made a public profession of faith but recognize their baptism as a part of their faith journey, is that recognized by members of our church, or would they have to be rebaptized?

@ BaptismAhead.org: Share your questions about baptism, as well as stories of what you feel when you are baptized. You can also blog about Scriptures and questions from the chapter and interact with others online.

LiViNg Faith

You live your faith by sharing your faith with others, showing them how joyful you are. —Emily, age 11

I could definitely do better. I need to work on using my free time wisely. I occasionally have my quiet time with God, but I want to improve so much. —Allison, age 14

I want the church to be more active in telling people that Christianity is more than just being good. —Jordan, age 13

- What are we to do once we come out of the waters of baptism?
- What do we expect, and what is expected of us?
- What are worship and Communion about?
- What are signs of life in your personal and communal faith?

Key Terms
Invocation: A prayer inviting God to be present in the worship—and to stir or wake up our spirits to be aware of God's presence with us.

Living Faith

Ordinance: A custom or practice established as a valued tradition. Baptists believe that Jesus named two things as something we should do symbolically to remember him: baptism and Communion. Some churches call these practices sacraments.

▶ ▶ ▶

It was late, but Jamal couldn't sleep. He had been thinking about everything that had happened in the last few weeks at church, and especially with Ms. Marsha and Ava. He was brooding about it, staring up at the ceiling with his hands behind his head. Whenever his mom noticed him so deep in thought, a frown of concentration on his face, she would say, "What are you rooting around for, Jamal? What are you searching for in that head of yours?"

She happened to be walking by his open door, a basket of laundry in her arms. "Hey, bud, lights out!" But Jamal didn't move. He was lost in thought.

Mom came into his room. "Hon? Are you okay?"

Jamal breathed a heavy sigh. Silence. Then, in a quiet voice Jamal started to open up. "Mom, is it okay if I'm not ready to be baptized yet? I mean, I know you said it was my decision, but I also know that you really want me to."

His mom thought for a moment and then gently offered, "Well, yes, I want this for you, but it is absolutely your decision." She put the basket down and sat on the corner of his bed.

Jamal's mom took a deep breath and then went on, "A long time ago, when you were just a baby, I made a promise to God that I would raise you with the Word of God as my guide, and with the help of a church that would be like a family to you, so that when you were ready, you could freely choose to follow Jesus. But for this to be real, Jamal, you have to choose it, and then choose every day to live faithful to God."

Jamal thought about it for a moment and then said, "Well, I guess for a long time, I didn't understand why someone had to go under water, like some weird club initiation. I mean, I just didn't think you needed that in order to be a good person or to even be part of the church. Why do I have to go under water in front of people? What does that change?"

He went on, "But this week, Ms. Marsha said that it's not about the water, it's about my heart and about outwardly showing a change in my life and my commitment to try to live like Jesus. So now it has so much more meaning that I really want it to be right. I want it to mean something, and not just do it because other people want me to or because of what people of church will think of me."

Jamal's mom was smiling, with tears on her cheeks. She hugged him and whispered, "I'm proud of you, baby, and it's okay for you to choose when the time is right." He hugged her tight. His eyes were watering, too.

▶ ▶ ▶

The Priesthood of All Believers

But you are a chosen race, a royal priesthood, a holy nation, God's own people, in order that you may proclaim the mighty acts of him who called you out of darkness into his marvelous light.

Once you were not a people,
    but now you are God's people;
once you had not received mercy,
    but now you have received mercy.
(1 Peter 2:9-10)

Baptists believe in the priesthood of all believers. We are all ministers! Every person is called to ministry, called to faithfully serving as the hands and feet of Jesus in the world. As followers of Jesus, as God's people, as ones who have received mercy, we are called to live in a new way and offer our lives freely.

But wait a minute. What is a priest? Perhaps the simplest definition would be that a priest is a go-between, someone who officially represents the people before God and represents God for the common people. A priest would have authority to lead worship, pray, and interpret Scriptures for you and for everyone else.

The people of Israel were used to having priests. One of the families, or tribes, of Israel was dedicated to the priesthood. For years and years, priests served as the go-betweens between ordinary people and God. Individuals did not feel that they had direct access (connection) to God. And there were all kinds of rules and traditions that gave structure to this religious system.

We believe that Jesus changed the system—that is, Jesus changed our understanding of how God is at work in people's lives. Jesus taught us how to talk to God through prayer and promised that God's Spirit would be active in our lives.

As Jesus' disciples began to develop and form what we now know as the church, they were empowered by the Spirit. Each person was gifted and called to play a part in the formation of the church. Some were called and designated as preachers, some as teachers; others had the gift of hospitality or served the ministry of the church in other ways.

In Baptist churches today, we believe each person is gifted and called to serve God. Each person can connect directly with God and have a personal relationship with Jesus.

■ How do you see these beliefs lived out in your church? In worship? In mission and in all the work of the church? In community life and church leadership?

_____

_____

Baptism Ahead

▶ ▶ ▶

Before he had left home for the school bus, Jamal's mom had given him a sealed envelope with "Ms. Marsha" written on it. He had wondered what it was about as he bounced along the bus route, looking from the envelope in his hands to the window and the rainy streetscape outside. *Was it something about him? What could it be? Had he done something wrong? Was it about his not wanting to be baptized yet?* He was tempted to open the envelope and find out, but the bus had sloshed to a stop in front of the school, and everyone began to push past and out down the narrow aisle. He put the envelope into his backpack and sat silently, until everyone was off the bus.

Jamal grudgingly made his way down the aisle and down through the double doors. *Sploosh!* The puddle he stepped into took his mind off of the envelope. Jamal imagined that everyone else had bounced right over that pothole on their way off the bus, as he now had one dry and one soaked shoe. Step-*squish*-step-*squish*-step-*squish*, all the way into the building, to his locker, and toward first period.

His day did not improve, much like the gray and rainy weather outside. But his shoe eventually dried out, even though he had that wet skin feeling as a reminder all day long. Jamal was glad to survive another day at Kennedy Middle School, under the radar, unnoticed by most people as he kept to himself.

He was glad the rain was down to a sprinkle as he made the way from the bus stop to Bethel and into the dry hallway. As he made his way toward the big room, the welcome sounds of the little kids playing always seemed to brighten him up a bit.

For some reason, today he just wanted to play with some of the kids. He didn't head for the video game console, and he did not sneak out of the room. He headed straight for two of the younger boys who were constructing a wall, perhaps a fort, out of old cardboard building blocks that looked like they had been in the Bethel Baptist toy stash since the days of Nehemiah, or perhaps they were from the days of Joshua and the battle of Jericho. They were faded and worn when Jamal first played with them years ago as a little guy, great building blocks that had stood the test of time and hundreds of little hands and big imaginations.

He was just getting lost in play with the blocks and boys when Ava came over and interrupted. "Hey, Jamal! It's time for group!" *Already?* Jamal thought as he looked up at her with a squint, maybe a frown.

It was then that he noticed Ava had an envelope in her hand, just like the one in his backpack, with "Ms. Marsha" written on the front. *Maybe I'm not in trouble, at least,* he thought as he popped up from the makeshift walls of cardboard bricks. He was curious again about the envelope.

■ What do you think is in the envelope?
■ Have you ever had a squishy and gray day? What made your day feel any brighter?
■ How do you see Ava and Jamal sharing in ministry with other people? With each other?
■ How do you serve in ministry with other people?

▶ ▶ ▶

As Ava led the way into the church library, her usual smile brightened even more. "I wonder what we are doing today?" she asked. Jamal was interested, too, in his quiet way, as he peeked over Ava's shoulder.

Ms. Marsha had placed several items on the big table. There was a stack of greeting cards, pairs of brown cotton work gloves, a plate with bread on it and a cup filled with grape juice, a bucket filled with cleaning supplies, a hymn book, a Bible, a box of plastic trash bags, a picture album, and a box of plastic gloves stacked on top of what looked like kitchen aprons. In the center of all the items was a worn wooden box that looked familiar to Ava and Jamal.

Ms. Marsha came in behind the two. They were too curious about the items on the table to notice until she broke the silence. "What are all those things for?" she asked.

Jamal looked back at her and gave a half smile. "We were going to ask you. What's going on?"

Ms. Marsha winked at both of them and said, "I'm asking: what do *you* think all of these things are for?"

Ava thought for a moment and then said, "I was thinking that today was the day we were talking about what it meant to be disciples and church members, after baptism."

Ms. Marsha nodded and affirmed, "Right!"

Ava and Jamal looked at each other. Ms. Marsha chuckled good-naturedly and then offered, "Okay, I will give you a hint. Look up in your Bibles and read out loud Matthew 25, verses 35-40." Ava dove for her backpack. Jamal reached across to the Bible on the table and found the passage first.

"Hey, no fair!" Ava complained, but Ms. Marsha calmed her down as Jamal read the verses aloud.

► ► ►

Caring for God's Family

"I was hungry and you gave me food, I was thirsty and you gave me something to drink, I was a stranger and you welcomed me, I was naked and you gave me clothing, I was sick and you took care of me, I was in prison and you visited me." Then the righteous will answer him, "Lord, when was it that we saw you hungry and gave you food, or thirsty and gave you something to drink? And when was it that we saw you a stranger and welcomed you, or naked and gave you clothing? And when was it that we saw you sick or in prison and visited you?" And the king will answer them,

Living Faith

"Truly I tell you, just as you did it to one of the least of these who are members of my family, you did it to me." (Matthew 25:35-40)

■ What does Jesus mean by these words?

_____

_____

■ What does this challenge you to do as a follower of Jesus?

_____

_____

▶ ▶ ▶

"I'm still not sure I understand." Ava was looking intently at the table. "I think you are telling us that as followers of Jesus, we should be doing those kinds of things. But we're just kids. How can we feed the hungry? And you're not asking us to visit prisoners, are you?"

Ms. Marsha held up a hand to stop Ava's flood of questions. "Let's take one thing at a time. Jamal, pick any item on the table and see if you can tell me what it might have to do with how we live our faith and share in ministry."

"Okay, that's not too hard. I think the cup and the bread represent Communion." Jamal was feeling more and more confident.

Ms. Marsha nodded, "You are right, Jamal. Now, tell me something about what Communion means or how we share in Communion in worship."

"Well, I know we have Communion on the first Sunday of the month, because my mom helps with serving it, and sometimes I help her clean up after church." He thought for a moment and then continued, "At every Communion, Pastor Chris reads a Scripture and then says that everyone is welcome at the table, if they have received Jesus Christ as Lord and Savior."

Ms. Marsha patted Jamal on the shoulder. "Good, Jamal. Our church chooses to celebrate the ordinance of Communion on the first Sunday of every month. Sometimes we pass trays to serve the elements of bread and small cups of grape juice. In this way, each person serves another person and receives from another person, so we all share in the act of giving, receiving, and serving. At other times, people come forward and take a piece of bread and dip it into the cup. By coming forward, people are making a physical effort to offer themselves to God."

Ava raised her hand out of habit and asked, "Umm, what does *ordinance* mean?"

"That is another great question, Ava!" Ms. Marsha congratulated her. "Ordinance in this situation means something that is a custom or practice established as a valued tradition. Baptists believe that Jesus named two things as something we should do symbolically to remember him: baptism and Communion. Some churches call these practices sacraments, which is another fancy word for holy. The difference for Baptists is, we don't think of the water or bread or cup as holy in themselves. They are symbols that help us remember Jesus, the one who is holy."

▶ ▶ ▶

Communion

Read Mark 14:22-25, followed by 1 Corinthians 11:23-26. Then consider this quote: "We couldn't live without food. In a similar way, when we eat this bread and drink this juice at Communion, our spiritual lives are being nourished. In a way, Jesus is becoming more and more a part of who we are" (Franklin W. Nelson, *Bridges of Promise*, p. 97).

At Water's Edge

Living Faith

■ What does Communion mean to you? What questions do you have about Communion and how it is shared in your church?

_____

_____

_____

Communion engages our senses in worship. The smell of bread, the taste of grape juice (or wine), the touch of the plate or cup as we are served and as we serve others by passing the communion elements.

■ What might Communion within the community of faith—people you know and care about—help you to feel?

_____

_____

_____

► ► ►

Ms. Marsha looked at her watch and hopped up from her chair. "Okay, if we don't leave now, we will be late for our serving opportunity." Ava looked at Jamal, and Jamal shrugged. He asked, a little nervous, "S-s-serving opportunity?"

"Well, today's opportunity is a surprise. I contacted your parents for permission to keep you a little later than normal. I hope you both brought the permission forms I gave to your parents." Ms. Marsha continued to be mysterious, not quite answering their curious question.

And then, it was as though a light went on in Jamal's brain. "Oh! So that is what is inside the envelope!" He surprised himself with the surprise in his voice. And then he questioned, "A permission form? Where are we going?"

Ms. Marsha finally let them know. "Today, we are going to drive downtown and serve a meal at a soup kitchen. After we serve dinner, we'll help with clean up, and then we will share the leftover food with the other volunteers who are serving there tonight. And then I will drive you home."

It was Ava's turn to question. "Um, leftovers? I'm kinda picky about what I eat."

Ms. Marsha smiled and quoted, "'Therefore, do not worry about what you will eat, or what you will drink, or what you will wear...but strive first for the kingdom of God!' That's from Matthew, chapter 6."

Ava looked at Jamal again. He just shrugged again. They got up from their chairs and got ready to go.

Ms. Marsha led the way out of the library. "Let's go! Oh, and grab the plastic gloves and aprons. We'll be needing those!"

Jamal stopped in his tracks. "Aprons?" He moaned and mumbled as he trailed behind the others down the hallway.

As they drove downtown in the church van, they continued their conversation. Ms. Marsha asked, "Remember the items on the table? Let's play a game and come up with different ways we can use those items in community ministry and what they may symbolize in our shared life of discipleship."

Jamal was looking out the window, feeling nervous about their destination and giving words to his feelings with a shrug and sarcasm. "Gee, that sounds fun."

Ms. Marsha melted his sarcasm with her warm smile. "Sounds like we have a volunteer! Jamal, you go first." Jamal's glare didn't last long. He respected Ms. Marsha too much to let it linger. He offered, "Well, I guess we need the gloves and aprons for serving food today. So, I guess that serving is a part of discipleship."

"Good! Serving others is an important part of discipleship. And there are many ways we can serve God and one another." Ms. Marsha looked back in the rearview mirror and cued Ava. "Okay, Ava! Your turn!"

Ava was quick to respond, as always. "I remember the wood box in the center of the table. Isn't that the prayer box that is usually at the back of the sanctuary? During worship, people are invited to write down prayer concerns on cards and put them in the box." And then Ava paused. "But who gets the cards?"

"Ava, that is a good question." Ms. Marsha was slowing down, making sure the lane was clear for a left turn. Then she went on, "After church, a volunteer from the prayer team checks the box. Then they share the cards with me and with the rest of the prayer team, usually by e-mail, because it is the fastest way we have to pass on information without having a meeting every week. If the person who wrote the concern marks on the card that they wish it to be shared with the whole church, we do that through our weekly e-mail update or through the prayer chain phone call tree. And for on-going concerns, we list those in the worship bulletin. We also have a prayer time at church on Thursday nights, and anyone is welcome to come to that and share in prayer."

Ava thought for a moment. "I never knew that so many people were involved other than Pastor Chris. That's really cool!" And then, curiously, "If I gave my e-mail to you, could I be included in the prayer mailings?"

Ms. Marsha nodded, "Of course!"

"All right, Jamal, your turn again."

He thought for a moment and then said, "I remember on the table the cup and bread for Communion, which we talked about, and there was a Bible and a song book. Were those there for worship?"

"Certainly the Bible is a core part of our worship as together we explore and respond to God's living Word." Ms. Marsha paused. "But before I talk about worship, I have questions for both of you. When, where, and how do you worship? And with whom do you worship? And how is worship meaningful for you?"

Jamal responded first. "Well, we worship on Sunday morning at church." He looked away but continued, "I like it when we sing the new songs. A lot of the old songs put me to sleep. I gotta admit, there are some days I'd stay in bed if my mom let me. No offense, to you or Pastor Chris!"

Ms. Marsha nodded as she prepared to turn into a parking lot, waiting for traffic to clear in front of them. "Jamal, you are right. There are some parts of our worship service that seem to put people to sleep."

Jamal was surprised to hear the teacher say such a thing!

Ms. Marsha continued, "But I hope you will understand that in worship, we try to do different things, including singing both old and new songs, in order to help people of all ages to participate and worship from the heart. We should worship because we *want* to, because when worship takes place out of obligation, is it really worship?"

Ava and Jamal looked at each other. There was a silence in the van as Ms. Marsha made the turn and then parked the vehicle. She turned back to Ava and Jamal and asked, "What does it mean for us to worship God 'in spirit and truth'?"

That was a hard question to answer as they sat in the van. Ava attempted to answer. "Well, you just said we should worship because we want to. I guess that if God knows our thoughts and our feelings, then it means we should be honest. You know, not just go through the motions, but really participate, and not just because our parents tell us to pay attention."

Jamal spoke next. "I'm starting to see a connection. You have helped us learn about things we should do as followers of Jesus, you know, like love others, and pray and study the Bible. But not like they are chores. We are *free* to, to *want* to be faithful."

Ms. Marsha was impressed. "You both are amazing! And yes, you are free. Free to worship, free to serve, free to live your faith as you feel directed by God, and free to share the journey with a faith community of other people. Now, we better get inside and get ready to serve the meal. And here is a question to think about while we work. Do you think that serving others can be an act of worshipping God? Think about it, and we'll talk about that on the way home."

As they headed into the soup kitchen, Jamal asked, "So remember how we are *free*? Does that mean I am free to not wear this apron?"

Ms. Marsha laughed. "Sorry, Jamal. That is one rule that the food service considers a holy command!"

■ Read John 4:23-24 with your adult mentor. Then briefly describe worship at your church.
■ What does it mean for you to worship "in spirit and in truth"?
■ Now think about other events, activities, and service or mission opportunities in your church. How is the work of the church worshipful? How does the work of our hands and hearts honor God?

► ► ►
Weird Worship Words and Explanations
■ *Prelude (and Postlude):* Pre- means "before," so this is music played before the service begins that is meant to set a quiet mood and help people focus as they gather for worship. *Post-* means "after," and this music gives you a quiet moment to reflect on the sermon or worship experience before you go out into the world.
■ *Invocation:* To invoke means to "invite" or "stir up." The invocation is a prayer inviting God to be present in the worship—

and to stir or wake up our spirits to be aware of God's presence with us.

■ *Intercessory prayer:* To intercede means to step in for, or to "represent." Some churches call this the pastoral prayer, or the prayers of the people. Usually, one voice is praying publicly, representing the joys and concerns of the community, asking for God's presence or healing in people's lives and in community and world concerns.

■ *Amen:* The English translation of this word is "so be it." At the end of a prayer, it says that we want the prayer to be answered. In many church traditions, people will also say "amen" when they agree with the preacher or feel moved by a word or song.

■ *Sermon:* You might think it's boring, but the sermon is intended to answer the important question: "How is God speaking to us today?" The preacher's message might explain Scripture or challenge listeners to respond with a particular action. The word *sermon* comes from a Latin word that means "discourse" or "conversation." (What if your church had more of a conversation during worship? What would it be like to ask questions and share your thoughts about the Scriptures and how you sense God speaking to us today?)

■ *Offertory:* The offertory is the time in a worship service when we respond to God through giving our financial resources. Giving back to God is also an important spiritual discipline for us to practice, giving first to God through the church offering but also learning how to live generous lives.

■ *Communion:* Other churches call this ceremony of the church the Eucharist or the Lord's Supper. In this ritual, the bread (or wafer) and wine (or grape juice) represent Jesus' body and blood. In Communion, we remember Jesus' life and death and resurrection. The word *Communion* includes and combines two meaningful words: "common" and "union." As we share this together, we hold Christ in common with one another and are united together.

Living Faith

■ *Benediction: Bene-* means "good" (like in beneficial), and *-diction* means "word" (like in dictionary). At the end of a worship service, the pastor sends us out into the world as with a "good word" that accompanies us as we step out together in faith.

▶ ▶ ▶

It was getting late, and their work at the soup kitchen was finished. Ava and Jamal were tired, and their hands were wrinkled from wearing plastic gloves to serve food and then helping with the dishes in the back of the big kitchen. Neither had ever worked that hard, and in a span of only two hours! Both of them had affected by the experience of serving, in ways they could not explain with words.

They somberly headed toward the church van in the parking lot. The cold of night was settling on the city. As Ava looked out of the window of the van, she noticed, back in the alley, a man digging through a trash can. Even from a distance she could see he had layers of dirty, tattered clothes on to keep warm.

"Hey! That man came through the food line! I remember him." Ava was thoughtful. "I wonder where he'll sleep tonight."

Ms. Marsha drove out of the parking lot and onto a mostly empty street. "There are many this night that we served that will sleep in the cold. Unfortunately, there are not enough beds in the shelters for all of our neighbors."

"Neighbors?" Jamal questioned. "I mean, I'm sorry that man is homeless, but I think of my neighbors as the people who live on my block. How can I be a neighbor to a stranger?"

Ms. Marsha's eyes met Jamal's through the rearview mirror as she drove. "Well, Jamal, who do you think that Jesus wants us to love? Can you think of any stories where Jesus talks about neighbors?"

He was silent. Ava waited and then started to put her hand up. Right then, Jamal timidly offered, "You're thinking about the Good Samaritan, right?"

▶ ▶ ▶
The Rule to Live

Just then a lawyer stood up to test Jesus. "Teacher," he said, "what must I do to inherit eternal life?" He said to him, "What is written in the law? What do you read there?" He answered, "You shall love the Lord your God with all your heart, and with all your soul, and with all your strength, and with all your mind; and your neighbor as yourself." And he said to him, "You have given the right answer; do this, and you will live."

But wanting to justify himself, he asked Jesus, "And who is my neighbor?" (Luke 10:25-29)

Jesus tells the man, "Do this, and you will live." You have most likely heard and know these words as the great commandment. In a slightly different telling of this story in the book of Matthew, it is Jesus who quotes these rules to live by and says that all other rules and laws point to these two: Love God, and love your neighbor (Matthew 22:37-40).

It is easy to quote these rules to live by. It is much harder to *live* them. The man questioning Jesus has to ask, "And who is my neighbor?" Is he asking if any person or particular group is *not* his neighbor? We tend to justify our behavior toward others in the same way. (The second part of this story in Scripture is the story Jamal was referring to, the story of the Good Samaritan in Luke 10:29-37. Jesus uses an example of a Samaritan, whom the Israelites listening to Jesus would have considered as an enemy or unclean person, and not as a neighbor. Read the story!)

At the center of who we are as followers of Jesus, we encounter this great commandment. All of our worship, Bible study, prayer life, devotion, mission work, care for friends and strangers, care for God's creation, everything we do as Christians connects to these commands. Easy rules to remember, not so easy to truly live. That is why it is called discipleship. Following Jesus is a disciplined effort of love, serving, learning, worship, and sharing life together. If we all lived by this rule of love, how much better could life be for all people?

■ How do you love God and love your neighbor? More importantly, how does fulfilling this rule make your life more alive? Write some of your thoughts here:

_____

_____

_____

_____

_____

▶ ▶ ▶

There was silence in the van as Ms. Marsha's words led all three toward reflections on the night at the soup kitchen. The lights of the city rushed by as they drove toward their warm and welcoming homes.

Jamal's house was the first stop on the way home. Ms. Marsha parked the van, but before he got out, she told them, "I want to thank you for your hard work tonight. I hope it was a new and eye-opening experience. I know I surprised you with it, and I won't do that again. Whenever we serve in mission and outreach as a church, I want you to know you are welcome to volunteer and choose how you will serve.

"Now, before you go, I know it's really late, and we did not get a chance to finish talking about the question I asked earlier, whether serving others can be an act of worshipping God. We'll continue that conversation some other time. There is so much more to our conversation about what it means to live faithfully as followers of Jesus. In fact, that is a conversation we can have for the rest of our lives!"

Ms. Marsha pulled two papers from the empty seat next to her and handed one to Ava and one to Jamal. He chuckled, "Let me guess…homework!"

With a knowing smile, Ms. Marsha responded, "I hope you have fun with this. It includes coming up with creative ways that we serve God and one another. Remember the items on the table? For instance, there were some greeting cards. What if we were to write cards to people who are unable to leave their home or people who are in hospitals and nursing homes? What if we were to write messages and send Bibles to prisoners through our team at church that visits the prison each month?"

Ava's eyes were getting really big. "I'm just overwhelmed. I have homework and dance class and school and chores at home."

"Oh, Ava, I don't mean for any of these suggestions to be *chores*." Ms. Marsha paused. "There are so many things that we can freely choose to do. No person can do all of these things alone. That is why we work together as a faith community. Together we can do so much more than we ever could alone. And you can choose what best fits you, how you feel called or led by God to serve others. It could include anything we already do, like caring for Mrs. Jenkins. Or it could include donating some of your clothes through the mission project our senior high youth are working on. Did you know that when people donate clothing, the most donated items are either for infants or adults, but children and youth in need are many times underserved, because items your size aren't donated as much?"

Ms. Marsha stopped. "Now my point is, those are just examples. Discipleship is not a list of chores. We don't check off mission, or volunteering, or worship, or Bible study. We don't get grades or extra credit from God for our work. All of these things are ways that we respond to God for God's love and grace in our lives. We do these things freely, out of love."

Jamal was nodding in agreement. "It's like Pastor Chris said in church one time—something like, 'We walk together, and sometimes we carry each other, and sometimes God carries us, and all we say and all we do, we do in love because God loves us.'" Jamal was sheepishly smiling. "See, I do pay attention in church!"

Ava was reading ahead on the homework page. "And so what is this part at the bottom about writing a rule as a Way of Life for us?"

"Well, Ava, that is something you may find helpful to do. Remember it is not a chore, but a way that you live something out. The rules should not be draining, but give more meaning to your living. Read the passages listed there, like the one from Matthew 22, with your parents, and maybe together you can have a conversation about how we live by God's rule!"

With that, they said goodbye to Jamal. Ms. Marsha waited for him to get inside the front door before driving Ava home.

▶ ▶ ▶

Other Churchy Words Explained

■ **Evangelism:** *Evangel* is a word used to describe a messenger (or angel) of God. The word *evangelism*, then, basically means "to share God news" or "good news." As followers of Jesus, we are challenged to share the Good News about Jesus with all people.

■ **Benevolence:** Remember that *bene-* means good? This word means having the ability to do good. It describes the mission work of the church in terms of serving people with needs, such as outreach to homeless or hungry people.

■ **Hospitality:** This word refers to showing kindness to guests and "strangers." How we treat each other is something that some cultures and groups take seriously. It can be as simple as offering a cup of cold water or saying (and meaning) "Welcome!"

■ **Deacon:** The word *deacon* comes from a Greek word meaning "servant." In the church, deacons (sometimes called elders) help the pastor with worship preparation and visiting church members. They may also help make important decisions in the church or serve as officers. (Read more in Acts 6:1-7 and 1 Timothy 3:8-13.)

■ **Laity:** This word means "of the people" and it refers to all church members who are not ordained as clergy (pastors). In Baptist churches in particular, the laity and clergy are all considered equally called as ministers. A lay leader may represent other church members as a committee officer, board chairperson, or moderator.

Homework

1. Make a list of other churchy words that you would like to explore. Research these terms in your Bible or a Bible dictionary, or by asking your pastor or adult mentor. You may also use a search engine online.

_____

_____

_____

_____

2. Read and reflect on Matthew 22: 37-40. Take time to pray and listen. How do you love God and love others?

_____

_____

_____

_____

3. What is your personal rule to live by? What guides your living and choices? Create your own Way of Life in the space provided.

_____

_____

_____

_____

@ **BaptismAhead.org:** You can share your list of churchy words and definitions, as well as your personal Way of Life.

CHAPTER 7

Now What?

If you could ask God a question…
What is it that I am put on the earth to do? —Jennifer, age 13

Even though I do not directly pray sometimes, do you know
that I am thinking of you and praising you, God?
—Stephanie, age 16

Can you please make our world a better place with people
that are kind and loving? —Natalie, age 12

- What questions do you have for God?
- What decisions have you made?
- Who can help you as you continue to navigate the path of faith?

Key Terms
Faith commitment: A discipline that you share with your faith community (church).
Covenant: A holy promise to God and others that you will live out.

Today was the last official day of the Baptism Ahead group. Ava was feeling rather melancholy about that. She was excited about being baptized soon but sad that the conversations with Ms. Marsha and Jamal were coming to an end. She wasn't sure how her relationship with Ms. Marsha would continue without a time set aside in the teacher's schedule just for her. And for Jamal. She was not sure if Jamal would ever talk to a girl unless he had to!

Ava arrived at Bethel Baptist a little early. She was surprised that Jamal was already there, too. Ms. Marsha was busy with some of the younger children in the big multi-purpose room, and it would be twenty minutes before their conversation would start in the library.

"Come here!" Jamal whispered (rather loudly for a whisper) and motioned to Ava from across the room. *Me? He's talking to me outside of class?* Ava thought. She was surprised. She headed over to Jamal.

"What's up?" she asked. He looked around, reminding her of some sort of spy in the movies. *What has gotten into him?* she wondered. Jamal only said, "We have T-minus 18 minutes. I want to show you something. Follow me!" And they sneaked down the darkened hallway toward the sanctuary.

Ava couldn't imagine where Jamal was taking her. Abruptly, he stopped and opened a door that Ava had never been through. They were in a small room or closet, and it was pitch dark when the door creaked shut behind her.

Then Jamal opened another door, and colorful light shone through. They were at the front of the sanctuary, at the doorway that Pastor Chris and the choir used to enter worship. The late afternoon sun was shining through the stained glass windows on the west wall. It was beautiful and peaceful to see the sanctuary this way, so different from Sunday morning.

"Come on, Ava! We need to hurry!" Jamal was moving quickly and silently up the center aisle. He went toward the back entrance on the right side, the door that Pastor Chris stood by to greet people after worship. *What is the big deal about this?* Ava thought.

It was in the entryway that Jamal veered right again, toward two wood panels covering the wall opposite the entrance. He turned and smiled at Ava, and then pushed on the left panel. There was a click, and a creak…the panel was a secret door!

"This is so cool!" Ava was almost giddy with excitement.

"Shh!" Jamal hushed her. "We don't have much time." He disappeared into the darkness, and Ava followed.

When her eyes adjusted once again to the dark, Ava saw that Jamal was already climbing up a steep, tight, spiral staircase. It twisted straight up in what felt like a dark tower. Ava scrambled behind him, up, up the dusty stairs.

When Jamal got to the top, he opened a large square hatch where the ladder-like stairs met the ceiling. Light was coming from above, and Ava could see much better now. As she emerged behind Jamal, she realized where she was—the top of the bell tower, right next to the big church bell!

"This is really cool!" Ava beamed. "How did you know how to get up here, Jamal?"

"Well, sometimes on Sunday, Pastor Chris asks me to pull on the rope downstairs that rings the bell. One time after church, my mom was helping clean up the Communion trays, and so I was playing around. I knew there had to be a way up to the top, but I had never seen any stairs. But that day, I saw Mr. Meadows, the janitor, pop the panel downstairs while he was cleaning up, and so when he left the sanctuary, I went back in and climbed up here. I've been coming up here ever since. It's so quiet up here. I used to hide out up here, but for the last several weeks, I've come up here to think, and, um…to pray and stuff."

Ava was surprised and flattered that Jamal had brought her up here, but she had to ask, "Jamal, I'm really glad you showed me this place. But if this is your secret place, why did you share it with me?"

Jamal was looking away, out over the street below. "I don't know...I guess I just couldn't keep it to myself. You can look out and see things, but they don't look like they do on the ground. I just feel close to God up here." Jamal looked right at her. "I've been seeing things differently after these past weeks with the discovery group." He paused. "You know, just because I don't say much out loud doesn't mean I'm not thinking about stuff like that. I guess I just wanted you to know."

"Jamal, I'm really glad you shared this with me. Thank you." Ava blushed a little.

Then she asked, "So are you ready to get baptized?"

Jamal squirmed and turned away. "I think we better head back before anyone notices we're gone. Maybe we can come back again later."

He headed for the stairs. Ava called after him, "Jamal, wait!" But he was already on the way down.

▶ ▶ ▶
Decisions and Possibilities

As we enter this chapter in Jamal's and Ava's story, Jamal does not yet seem ready to make a faith commitment for baptism, while Ava seems that she has been ready for a while to take this step of faith.

■ At this point, who do you identify with more? Why do you feel this way?

_____

_____

_____

Baptism Ahead

You need to know that it is normal (and definitely okay!) for you and your friends sharing the experience of Baptism Ahead to be at different places on your faith journey. You may have friends who seem further ahead of you in their decisions and commitments. Perhaps you are not yet ready for baptism. Perhaps a friend of yours does not feel ready for the commitments that you feel ready for.

■ How might you support one another, even if you are at different places on the path of faith?

_____

_____

_____

You are free to make choices and faith decisions. These steps of faith must be yours, not pushed or forced by any other; they must be authentically your choices.

■ What faith decisions have you made at this point in your journey in terms of your commitment to follow Jesus? In your involvement with the church? Who can you talk with about your commitments?

_____

_____

_____

Take the time to discuss the following questions with a parent, mentor, teacher, or pastor. Write your responses and reflections to these questions in the space provided:

Now What?

■ Are you ready to publicly share your commitment to receive Jesus as Lord and Savior? _____

■ Are you ready to be baptized? _____

■ Are you ready to be an active member of a church, committed to participating in the life and ministry of a faith community? _____

■ What other commitments are you considering, such as a call to becoming a pastor or missionary? _____

■ What are some questions you still have that might affect your decisions and any possible outcomes? _____

■ If you are not yet ready to follow Jesus into the waters of baptism and in a life of discipleship, will you continue to explore these choices freely, with the guidance of an adult mentor? _____

▶ ▶ ▶

Ava could not understand Jamal. One moment, he was excited to show her his secret fortress of solitude, and the next moment he would not even look her in the eye. As soon as she asked a personal question, he was gone. She was out of breath climbing down from the bell tower, and he was nowhere to be seen.

Ava headed back for the library. When she arrived, there was Jamal, spinning in his favorite chair but looking at the floor. Ms. Marsha was warm and welcoming, as always. "Ava! Here we are again, the three of us, and God is present with us!"

Ms. Marsha lit a candle and said, "Let this flame be a silent reminder that the Light of the world is with us! God was with us before we came here, God was waiting for us to arrive, God is present in our words and actions, and God will go with us into the days ahead.

"Today is the last day of our Baptism Ahead group." Ms. Marsha seemed serious. "Now I know that this is not goodbye. We three will have other opportunities to share questions of faith and to share life together in worship, in mission, and in the community that is our church family. But this has been a special time set aside for us to explore together."

Ms. Marsha then shared from what was becoming a familiar Scripture to Ava and Jamal. "From the fourth chapter of Paul's first letter to Timothy. Paul the teacher shared these words with Timothy the student as they became partners in ministry and encouraged one another as followers of Jesus. He said, 'Let no one despise your youth, but set the believers an example in speech and conduct, in love, in faith, in purity....Give attention to the reading of scripture, to exhorting, to teaching. Do not neglect the gift that is in you...put these things into practice, devote yourself to them...so that all may see you grow in faith.'"

Both Ava and Jamal were listening intently as Ms. Marsha continued, "You both have the free choice to proclaim Jesus as your Lord and Savior and to follow Jesus with your daily choices along the journey of life. Know that there are many in this faith community who will guide and support you and love you no matter when, where, or how you respond to God's invitation." She paused and then asked, "Is there any decision that you would like to share here and now?"

Ava was quick to volunteer. "I want to follow Jesus! I want to tell the world that Jesus is my Savior, and I want to enter the waters of baptism." Ms. Marsha hugged Ava with one arm, giving her a silent nod, her face filled with pride for Ava.

With her other hand, Ms. Marsha reached out and patted Jamal's folded hands on the table. "Jamal? Would you be willing to share with us what you are feeling?"

Silence.

Finally, Jamal looked up and quietly said, "I'm grateful for this group. I love this church. I...I've decided to...um, I'm not ready to, well, I feel I still have a lot of questions, and I'm just now feeling really able to ask them."

Ms. Marsha hugged Jamal, just as she had hugged Ava. Her face was filled with pride for him, just as it was for Ava. Ms. Marsha's words were a gift of grace. "Jamal, just know that God loves you and is with you and for you, as you come to know God and make faith commitments in your own time. And we're with you and for you, too!"

"I have a gift for each of you." Ms. Marsha reached over to the bookshelf behind her and gave each of them a small white candle inside a glass holder. "It is my hope that you will light this candle in your own quiet times, as a reminder of what we shared in this journey of discipleship and discovery, and that we continue to share the journey of faith. As you pray and read your Bible, may this candle be a reminder that the Light of the world is the living Word of God that is present with each of us."

Ms. Marsha closed their time together with a simple prayer. "God, thank you for your presence in the life we share as a community of faith. Help us to more fully know and love you as we grow in faith. Help us to more fully know and love one another. Thank you for your trust, understanding, love, and grace. In Jesus' name we pray, and we live. Amen."

And so, the Baptism Ahead group came to an end. And there was so much more yet to share! But perhaps it was simply a new beginning of their relationship with one another as a part of a community of faith, a church family, in many ways like yours. Discuss the following questions with your adult mentor.

■ How will you continue to explore questions of faith, study the Scripture, and live your faith?
■ How will you continue the journey of faith, like Ava and Jamal?
■ Read Galatians 6:2 and Colossians 3:12-17. What does it mean to help one another with our burdens?
■ What does it mean for you to live a new life in Christ as described in Colossians?

▶ ▶ ▶

Ava said goodbye and headed home. It wasn't quite 6 p.m., and Jamal was waiting for his mom to pick him up. He had time to linger, whether he wanted to or not. Ms. Marsha stopped him before he left the library. "Jamal, I was hoping for a word with you alone."

Now what? he wondered, holding his breath. Ms. Marsha smiled and said, "One of our traditions at Bethel Baptist is to give children and youth a Bible of their own. I have noticed that during these weeks you have not had your own Bible with you for our conversations and have been happy to let you use one of mine."

Jamal could feel his ears getting hot. He stumbled on his words. "Well, I…I'm embarrassed to say. The one I got in third grade…I do have it. At home. But, it's really for little kids. I…uh, well, it has little pink and blue sheep on the cover…" His words trailed off.

Ms. Marsha smiled a knowing smile. "I thought it might be something like that. Anyway, I want to say that you are really maturing, and I believe you are on the edge of some important questions and decisions in your life. So, as a way of helping you continue the journey, I wanted to give you this."

Ms. Marsha held out a new Bible to Jamal. It did not have sheep on the cover. Instead, it had his name, etched in the corner. Jamal was speechless.

Silently, he reached for it. "Wow. Thank you," was all he could say. He held it close. It had a leather cover. *It even smelled grown up*, he thought.

Jamal gave Ms. Marsha a hug. She said, "Well, I hope this will be something you can use, as you continue to navigate the path of faith, and as you consider what it means to follow Jesus. And remember, you can always come to me or Pastor Chris with questions about anything, including baptism and what it means to be a part of the faith community."

"Thank you. Thank you!" Jamal was grateful. He seemed to walk out of the room lighter than when he had entered, even though he had added a Bible and a candle to the load in his backpack. He felt full of love. He felt free.

▶ ▶ ▶
Freedom in Christ

For freedom Christ has set us free. Stand firm, therefore, and do not submit again to a yoke of slavery....For you were called to freedom, brothers and sisters; only do not use your freedom as an opportunity for self-indulgence, but through love become slaves to one another. For the whole law is summed up in a single commandment, "You shall love your neighbor as yourself." (Galatians 5:1,13-14)

You are free! You are responsible for you. How then, shall you choose to live? How will you respond to the One who has set you free? How do you choose to live toward others with love?

Pray and reflect with your mentor one more time on the gift and responsibility of freedom.

■ Consider the rest of Galatians 5:22-26. How may you choose to live by the Spirit? What does it mean to belong to Jesus?

_____

_____

_____

▶ ▶ ▶

It was a beautiful Sunday morning. The crisp, cool dawn was warmed by the light of the sun. Jamal and his mom walked to church together. He was even quieter than usual. Perhaps he was rooting about something.

When they entered the sanctuary, Jamal quickly moved to a pew in the back. The worship service began as usual, with a time of announcements and a time of greeting and a time of prayer, yet through all of the opening time in worship, Jamal seemed distracted. When the congregation stood to sing, Jamal only stared forward, gazing curiously at the light through the open baptismal window above the singing choir.

After everyone sat down, Pastor Chris appeared in the baptistery, beaming ear to ear. "Dear friends, this is a beautiful day. For today we celebrate new life as one of our young friends follows the example of Jesus and enters the waters of baptism. For when we proclaim Christ as our Lord and Savior, we die to our old self and are raised to walk in newness of life."

Pastor Chris turned and held out a hand. The congregation was hushed, and you could hear a small slosh of water as a hand reached out to grab Pastor Chris's hand. Ava came into view! Jamal thought she looked a little nervous but also very happy. Ava's family sat in the front row of the church. Her dad snapped a picture.

Then Pastor Chris said, "Ava Elizabeth Diesto, do you believe in Jesus Christ as your Lord and Savior?" Boldly, Ava spoke out so that all could hear. "Yes! I do!"

Pastor Chris took hold of Ava and said, "Then upon your profession of faith, we your church family celebrate your baptism, in the name of our Creator God, our Savior Jesus, and the Holy Spirit." With those words, Pastor Chris gently dipped Ava back into the glistening water.

With a whoosh, Ava emerged from the water, a wave of water and tears of joy dripping from her face. Pastor Chris looked into Ava's eyes and proclaimed, "Ava Elizabeth, you are God's beloved child!" Then Pastor Chris turned toward the congregation and said, "People of God, welcome your sister in Christ!" And the crowd gave a great cheer.

Now What?

At that moment, Brian, the fifth grader Jamal remembered as the kid who got water up his nose, went to the table in front of the pulpit and lit a candle. It was a tradition and an honor at Bethel Baptist for the last person to be baptized to light a candle to celebrate the new life of the next person to be baptized. Jamal watched closely as Brian lit the candle, focused on the growing and warm light of the flame.

Pastor Chris then gave an invitation. "A candle has been lit in celebration of new life. And yet you will see that there is another candle that remains unlit, for there is still room in God's family for more…for *you*…for all. The choice to follow Christ is yours. Perhaps today, someone here would like to come forward and join this church family or make a public profession of faith and follow Jesus in the waters of baptism and in a commitment of discipleship. O Lord, may your kingdom come, on earth as it is in heaven."

Jamal gazed from the glowing candle celebrating Ava's baptism, toward the unlit candle, back and forth. He felt a stirring in his stomach…no, it was in his heart, his soul. He felt warmth from within, like a light, like a flame.

He was happy for his friend, and yet he was unsettled. What could he do? What should he do? What would he do?

▶ ▶ ▶

Does Jamal go forward in the worship service to proclaim Jesus as Lord and Savior and request baptism? Does he wait? What happens next for Jamal? Perhaps you can help Jamal with his decision. You can write an ending to this story, and tell others part of your faith story.

The adventure has only just begun, and God is with us on the journey!

@ **BaptismAhead.org**: You can vote online for a response from Jamal and write your own baptism story. You can ask and answer questions of faith with other youth and interact with the author as we continue to explore together what it means to follow Jesus.

Homework

1. A covenant is a holy promise. With the person or group you have been reading and sharing the experience of Baptism Ahead with, make a holy promise to support one another on the journey of faith. How will you support one another and share the journey?

2. Write this promise down for each person to have a copy. You can also add words of affirmation for one another. You might want to make this promise into a special bookmark for your Bible. That way, you will have a special reminder whenever you are reading.

Continue the adventure of walking together in the way of Jesus!